CEO School

"*CEO School* is the kind of concise, focused look at what works, and what doesn't, that busy leaders will appreciate. Invaluable lessons from those who've lived it."
—General Stanley McCrystal, *former Commander, US Joint Special Operations Command (JSOC), author of the New York Times bestseller* Team of Teams

"Reading through the book made me feel: I've been there, I have done that, but I wish I had read this book before."
—Arzu Aslan, *CEO of Tat Food, Turkey*

"This thought-provoking book challenges some fundamental assumptions about what makes business leaders effective. Fascinating read!"
—Marshall Goldsmith, *Thinkers 50 #1 Leadership Thinker in the World and author of the #1 New York Times bestseller* Triggers

"The authors have provided us with new and interesting angles on how to reach the top and then stay there, carefully crafted in the style of an easy conversation with a wise mentor."
—Kevin Murray, *ex-CEO, executive coach and bestselling author of* The Language of Leaders *and* Communicate to Inspire

Stanislav Shekshnia • Kirill Kravchenko
Elin Williams

CEO School

Insights from 20 Global Business Leaders

Stanislav Shekshnia
INSEAD
Fontainebleau, France

Kirill Kravchenko
Gubkin Oil and Gas University
Moscow, Russia

Elin Williams
Oxford, UK

ISBN 978-981-10-7864-4   ISBN 978-981-10-7865-1   (eBook)
https://doi.org/10.1007/978-981-10-7865-1

Library of Congress Control Number: 2017963366

This Palgrave Pivot imprint is published by Springer Nature
The registered company is Springer Nature Singapore Pte Ltd.
The registered company address is: 152 Beach Road, #21-01/04 Gateway East, Singapore 189721, Singapore

PREFACE: WHY NOT A CEO SCHOOL?

"You should start a CEO School," said a voice from the back of the class.

This happened during an ordinary session in a traditional leadership programme for executives at a top international business school. The first author was teaching a topic that he'd covered many times before. So he was surprised when one of the participants challenged him with a brand-new idea.

"Running a company is a profession, just like medicine or flying an aircraft," she continued. "You should be able to train people for that."

The intrigued leadership professor (who had been a CEO) called his friend and colleague, the second author (who—as it happens—was still a CEO), and a single idea began to grow into a whole bunch of questions....

Is "CEO" really a profession like any other? Should there be qualifications and exams? If so who would the examiners be? What essential skills and knowledge should be covered by the curriculum? Would this need to be adapted to different countries and cultures? What kind of continuing professional development would be required? Conversely, what are the "no-nos": the things that CEOs should *never* do?

Last but not least, who were the best people to answer all these questions?

Who better, we thought, than a carefully assembled selection of truly top international CEOs from the G20 nations: the world's 20 biggest economies? And over the next few years we set out to interview one accomplished business leader from each of them.

Wherever we went, we tried to choose someone with a proven *track record*, not just the position of CEO. We didn't limit ourselves to any particular type of company either. Our sample included family businesses, founder-led enterprises, partially state-owned organisations and publicly traded corporations. But in each case, we tried to find an industry that the country concerned was particularly known for on the international business stage. For China and Germany we selected manufacturing, for Japan – electronics, Russia – energy, Italy – fashion, Spain – football... and so on. We couldn't cover every industry or type of organisation, of course. This is certainly not a statistical study. We have no banks or agribusiness in our list, to name just a couple of obvious omissions. But we're happy with the broad balance of the final selection, which includes an airline and a beverage company, as well as two globally renowned corporations: General Electric (GE) and BP.

It was a great privilege to meet all of these extraordinary leaders. We learned a lot simply from being in their presence as well as from their answers to our questions. As for these answers, some were expected and others quite unorthodox. But one thing was clear. CEOs have a different take on leadership than experts in business schools. They use different language and have a distinctive perspective that, we believe, needs to be passed on. Rather like a "school of philosophers," our interviewees have a way of seeing their role that others have much to learn from—especially those who wish to follow in their footsteps.

That's why, in the end, we decided we wouldn't start a school *for* CEOs but write a book, based on the insights that emerged from our interviews. And we present our findings in the form of seven easy-to-read "masterclasses". By way of summary, our table of contents should be self-explanatory. The chapters will take you, respectively, through the personality, education, experience, skills, roles, style and mastery of challenges required of a successful CEO. The book is also ordered to correspond roughly to the CEO lifecycle—from early years to retirement—with the caveat that it's never too early (or too late) to glean learning from any section.

Ultimately, we figured we could reach more people by publishing a book than by starting a school... which leads to yet another question: who is the book you're holding in your hand designed for?

Well, most obviously, this book is for wannabe CEOs—from high-school students to senior executives. We reckon the pages that follow will be of particular interest to MBA students or candidates embarking on any kind of leadership training for business.

But we also have another audience in mind—and that's educators of aspiring CEOs. We'd like our colleagues in business schools to look at their curricula and check that they're teaching the right subjects in the right way. We'd even like high-school teachers to read this book, as they're in a position to encourage and nurture the skills that will eventually take some of their current students to the top of great companies two or three decades from now. Come to think of it, why not kindergarten teachers too? After all, many future CEOs haven't started "big school" yet.

Given that education begins at home, we're also interested in reaching parents. Some of the traits described by our CEOs are acquired more easily at a very young age. Of course, you might think that bringing up your children to be top business leaders is crazy—not to mention irresponsible parenting. But what if these CEO attributes also turn out to be the basic recipe for a good life as an active citizen? And if you happen to run a *family* business, the question of whether your offspring will make good business leaders is not so crazy after all.

At the other end of the scale, another reader might be a board member, headhunter or HR director involved in recruiting CEOs. Maybe even CEOs themselves will be interested in the views of others in the same role, especially if they're putting together a succession plan.

Finally, *CEO School* is for any student of human nature—amateur or professional. If you're interested in what makes some people exceptional, read on.

But before you turn the page, take a moment to browse through our list of CEOs who agreed to share their wisdom with us. We're both proud and grateful that they gave us—and now you—their time and their insights. Think of this as a book, not with three authors, but 23 authors. As one of them, Constantino Galanis of Química Apollo (Mexico) says, "I've been a CEO for the last 25 years. I've learned a lot of things that I need to pass on to people. But, because of the nature of my work, I don't have time."

The 20 Additional Co-authors of *CEO School*
And the companies they led at the time of their interview

José Ángel Sánchez, Real Madrid (Spain, not a G20 member but representing the EU)
Abdel F. Badwi, Bankers Petroleum (Canada)
Renato Bertani, Barra Energia (Brazil)
Diego Bolzonello, Geox (Italy)
Peter Coleman, Woodside (Australia)
Bob Dudley, BP (UK)
Constantino Galanis, Química Apollo (Mexico)
Miguel Galuccio, YPF (Argentina)
Jeffrey Immelt, General Electric (USA)
Shuzo Kaihori, Yokogawa Electric Corporation (Japan)
Mazen Khayyat, El-Khayyat Group (Saudi Arabia)
Temel Kotil, Turkish Airlines (Turkey)
Chul-Kyoon Lee, Daelim Industrial Co. (Korea)
Stefan Messer, Messer Group (Germany)
Vladimir Rashevsky, SUEK (Russia)
Richard Rushton, Distell (South Africa)
Jean Sentenac, Axens (France)
Didie Soewondho, PT Wijaya Infrastruktur (Indonesia)
Nishi Vasudeva, Hindustan Petroleum Corporation (India)
Yang Wansheng, China Machinery Engineering Corporation (China)

See the end of the book for mini-biographies of all of the above—and the beginning of each chapter for proverbs from their respective countries.

The conversations with the 20 CEOs inspired most of the ideas and approaches presented in this book, but our thinking has been strongly influenced by many other people, their actions and their thoughts. Hundreds of business leaders from dozens of countries with whom we have worked as subordinates, colleagues, consultants, coaches, advisers and directors over the last three decades made indirect yet invaluable contributions to this book by giving us multiple opportunities to observe CEOs in action and sharing with us their views on how business leaders develop and what makes them effective. Our research has incorporated a number of leadership theories and concepts, notably the theory of personal attributes, the theory of leadership roles, the contingency view of leadership, power theory, leadership styles, agency theory and social capital theory.

That said, the work of two leadership theorists strongly shaped our thinking on leadership and the design of our research. First, the books and articles of Peter Drucker convinced us many years ago to look at what effective business leaders do rather than who they are, to search for a limited number of success factors in CEO performance and to appreciate the critical roles of practice and reflection in leadership development. Drucker insisted that good CEOs work for the organisation rather than for its stakeholders and create great companies that outlast their leaders. Second, Manfred Kets de Vries has conclusively demonstrated the effectiveness of a psychodynamic approach in understanding leadership performance and development. He emphasises the critical role of leadership experience in a CEO's development and especially the positive impact of dealing with early career adversity. Many years ago, Manfred introduced us to a clinical approach and mentored us in designing and conducting research interviews. He taught us to see the invisible and to hear the unsaid—which is, we hope, what makes our *CEO School* such a revealing read.

Fontainebleau, France   Stanislav Shekshnia
Moscow, Russia   Kirill Kravchenko
Oxford, UK   Elin Williams

Acknowledgements

In addition to the 20 CEOs we interviewed for this project—effectively co-authors whose contribution cannot be overestimated—many people and organisations have helped us to dream, research, write and publish this book. We would like to express our gratitude to them all.

First and foremost, we would like to thank our institutional supporters, particularly INSEAD and NIS, for providing financial and other resources to enable our research.

Denis Korepanov from NIS was our right hand in researching CEOs and their companies, reaching out to them to schedule meetings and finding other useful material. Without him this book would have never taken shape. We would also like to thank Nadezda Kokotovic, Vedrana Lukic and Zoran Tavzes from NIS for their enormous help with researching, organising, scheduling, transcribing interviews and making valuable content suggestions.

Many colleagues from academia have given us feedback and advice after reading parts of the manuscript or listening to our ideas. We would like to thank Professors Alena Ledeneva (UCL), Manfred Kets de Vries (INSEAD), Subi Rangan (INSEAD), Phil Anderson (INSEAD) and Valery Yakubovich (ESSEC).

We are very grateful to our clients, partners and friends from the business world who helped us to develop the concepts presented in this book by listening, sharing and critiquing. Among them are George Abdushelishvili, Oleg Bagrin, Gregory Fedorishin, Pavel Kiryukhantsev, Kirill Matveev, Dmitry Vasilkov, Oleg Polyakov, Ekaterina Ryasentseva,

Alexander Saveliev, Sergey Sirotenko, Oleg Smirnov, Murat Ülker, Vitaly Vassiliev, Vadim Yakovlev and Sergey Vorobiev.

Veronika Zagieva, Alexandra Matveeva and Alexey Ulanovsky from Ward Howell International provided invaluable assistance with data and recommended reading, and served as sounding boards for some of the ideas we would later present in this book.

Our assistants Nastassia Zorina, Aurelia Merle, Tatiana Shuvalova, Alfred Renshaw and Dragana Nikitovic ensured we had time to work on the book, scheduled appointments and kept us in good spirits.

Finally, our thanks go out to Vishal Daryanomel and Anushangi Weerakoon at Palgrave, whose editorial and production wizardry miraculously transformed our words into the book you are about to read.

CONTENTS

ABOUT THE AUTHORS

Kirill Kravchenko is Deputy CEO for Organizational Affairs of Gazprom Neft. For eight years, until March 2017, he was CEO of Serbian multinational oil company, NIS, where he remains on the board of directors. He previously worked as a consultant and for YUKOS and Schlumberger in Europe and Latin America. He has a degree in sociology (Moscow State University) and PhD in economics (Dmitry Mendeleev University of Chemical Technology of Russia).

Stanislav Shekshnia is a professor of Entrepreneurship and Family Business at INSEAD and a senior partner at Ward Howell International. He provides advice and coaching to senior executives, holds several board memberships and was previously CEO of Alfa-Telecom and Millicom International Cellular. This is his ninth book. Professor Shekshnia was educated at Moscow State University (master's and PhD) and Northeastern University (MBA).

Elin Williams is a freelance writer specialising in business, careers and higher education. She holds a BA and doctorate from the University of Oxford and is a qualified teacher.

LIST OF FIGURES

CHAPTER 1

Class 1: Introduction—Getting Ready for School

Abstract Before school starts, we'd like to define some common ground. The CEO is the most senior executive in the company. He or she oversees the business and makes key decisions within the framework of authority given to him or her by the board of directors. So what makes a good CEO? Our experts agree that a good CEO has a sufficient (five to seven years) track record of delivering superior operational and financial performance (beating industry competition and delivering returns to shareholders), creates a solid foundation for the business's growth in the long run, prepares a successor and leaves a positive legacy that outlasts his or her tenure. The 20 experts agree that this all adds up to a very challenging task, but from their experience they know that it's not impossible.

They also agree among themselves and with many academics that there can be no such thing as a standard curriculum with a final professional exam in a "CEO School." So don't expect our CEO School to be a simple "how to" guide or a step-by-step recipe for success. Rather, it is a well-curated collection of expert insights supported by research findings to apply to your own experiences and leadership development strategies. After all, the job of CEO is a job like no other. So our CEO School was always going to be a school like no other.

Keywords CEO • Good CEOs • CEO development • CEO performance • CEO succession

© The Author(s) 2018
S. Shekshnia et al., *CEO School*,
https://doi.org/10.1007/978-981-10-7865-1_1

1

Aller Anfang ist schwer. (Germany)
Meaning: All beginnings are hard.

As with most learning, you'll get more out of our *CEO School*, if you do a little pre-reading. And, as with most books, we won't begin at the beginning but before it. Let's get the essential background and key facts and figures out of the way first, so that we can all start learning in the same place and from the same base. But before we even do that, let's take a look at a job ad.

> **Wanted: An Outstanding Professional Leader**
> **Skills:** Must be a gifted communicator who knows exactly when to stop communicating and start taking action. Only big-picture thinkers with an eye for detail need apply. Also must be able to see clearly into the future, so as to deliver both short- *and* long-term gains for investors and all other stakeholders. (Note: please supply your own crystal ball.) Essential to be able to spot, nurture and challenge talent. (Note: please supply your own mind-reading equipment.)
>
> **Experience:** You are a proven financial and strategic wizard who is prepared to take risks—but not in a risky kind of a way. In addition, you know absolutely everything about the business—but without thinking you know everything (which would be disastrous). You have changed jobs at least ten times and worked in multiple geographies and functions—but must be able to demonstrate continuity of experience.
>
> **Attributes:** This is a job for a gregarious team player, well fitted to coping with the loneliness of life at the top. Applicants should also have ruthless empathy, expert common sense, rigorous creativity and unerring good luck. The successful candidate can expect a punishing schedule of long hours and global travel, during which he or she will be expected to exhibit boundless and indefatigable energy.
>
> **Salary:** Will attract relentless attention for being too high.

Yes, the role of the Chief Executive Officer (or, depending on where you're sitting, Managing Director, President, Head Honcho or just plain Big Boss) is challenging—if not downright self-contradictory at times. And the rewards, though usually generous, will be subject to endless scrutiny.

All the same, the title of CEO is much prized and has spread like wildfire through the English-speaking nations and beyond. It's a surprisingly young term, in fact. The first Chief Executive Officers popped up in mid-1950s' America, and by the mid-1970s, most heads of major US corporations were known, more familiarly, as CEOs. As the 1980s progressed, the good old pinstriped, bowler-hatted, pipe-smoking British Managing Director made way for a dynamic, thrusting new breed of "leader", and by the turn of the millennium, CEO was the dominant term on UK business cards too. Next stop the world.

1.1   WHAT'S A CEO ANYWAY?

Whatever you call it, the job we're talking about is basically that of the most senior manager *within* a company. It's distinct from the governance and oversight role taken by the *external* board of directors, although the CEO usually sits on the board and may also be its chair. Of course, this is an oversimplification of a global pattern that has many local variations—which explains why some of our 20 co-authors do not have the job title CEO. But simple is good enough for our purposes.

So much for defining a CEO. How do you define a *good* CEO? We agree with our co-authors that it takes a number of factors to make a good business leader. First, a good CEO needs to remain at the top for a significant period of time, if only because, otherwise, there wouldn't be enough data to judge his or her performance. As Vladimir Rashevsky of SUEK (Russia) told us: "You need at least seven years to leave your mark on a company."

Rashevsky comes from a country where a staggering 30% of CEOs of the largest companies leave within a year of starting their job. Things are probably a little better in America, where the median tenure of Fortune 1000 bosses in office in 2015 was 3.5 years, but the trend is downwards. The equivalent figure for 2010 was five years, and for 1980 it was seven years. In other words, CEO longevity is not what it used to be. Many business leaders just don't stay long enough to qualify for the label "good." Yet the ones who are good usually stay longer than Rashevsky's suggested seven years. The average tenure of "100 best-performing CEOs in the world" identified by Harvard Business Review in 2016 is 12 years.

Not that the length of tenure is everything. Richard Rushton of Distell (South Africa) told us: "I think that the very big danger with long-serving CEOs is that they start to believe their own stories—and that can be dangerous in a changing world. The longer you serve as CEO, the greater danger that you don't see the wood from the trees." As with all key performance indicators, the number of years in post should be treated with caution.

Second, no matter how long you stay in the job, you must systematically beat the competition and achieve superior operational and financial results to qualify as a good CEO. In his interview with us, Constantino Galanis of Química Apollo (Mexico) insisted:

> The most important factor has to be growth. And this growth should be higher than the average. Last year we had 35% growth, this year we also plan on 35% growth. This is what enables our company to get ahead, spend money on research and development or diversification. It's what enables us to generate new ideas—and bring them to the table and to the market. Even in downtimes we aim for healthy growth.

Third, you have to deliver superior returns to the shareholders of your company. And to do so on a continuous basis. Jeff Immelt's predecessor at GE Jack Welch became legendary for improving corporate earnings every quarter for most of his 20 years at the helm. Not all our CEOs manage to repeat his record, but they all recognise the crucial importance of this element of their performance.

Both operational performance and value creation for shareholders have to be sustainable in the long term, even if the concept of "long term" depends on where you're sitting geographically. As Chul-Kyoon Lee of Daelim Industrial Co. (Korea) observed, "We survived 77 years. In Korea very few companies are this old. And we are looking for another 120 years. As CEO, I need to have a corporate foundation for the future for both shareholders and for employees."

We believe that this "foundation for the future" perspective is crucial for understanding what makes a good CEO, and it adds the last—and probably most important—dimension to assessing achievement: effective succession. Good CEOs leave the company in good enough shape for their successor to carry on doing the same. When our INSEAD colleagues, Herminia Ibarra, Urs Peyer and Morten Hansen, first compiled the top 100 *Best-Performing CEOs in the World* for *Harvard Business Review* in 2010, based on long-term performance over entire length in post, they admitted that the "ultimate gold-plated list would comprise CEOs whose companies performed well not only during their tenure but after it." What's more, they noted that they could find very few cases of a highly ranked CEO passing the baton to a successor who was also highly ranked.

Effective succession clearly does not come automatically. For various reasons—from rational desire to keep power indefinitely to deep, dark, subconscious "fear of death" after leaving the top job—most CEOs are reluctant to engage in a comprehensive programme of succession planning and development. As former CEO of BP John Browne noted during an interview (a few years after stepping down): "Nobody leaves early enough... Try and remember that as you go through your tenure. I forgot it. I think a lot of people forget it. Remembering when to bow off the stage is more important than knowing when to go on the stage."

Of our 20 interviewees only a few were willing to talk about their succession planning. In fact, Abdel F. Badwi of Bankers Petroleum (Canada), who was actively engaged in finding a replacement for himself at the time when we met with him, spoke of the difficulty of finding and handing over to the right person. "We were in a search for a CEO, so this is very fresh in my mind," he sighed, when we asked him questions about the must-have attributes, skills, knowledge and experience of CEOs. But he didn't have any simple answers for us—and perhaps that would be too much to ask for at this stage—before his successor has proven himself.

So, instead of expert insights, here are two true stories to demonstrate what we mean by effective succession planning.

A Tale of Two Successions

Danaher is an American multinational corporation operating in the fields of design, manufacturing and marketing of industrial and consumer products. It's one of those companies most people have never heard of, but in 2015 it had a global workforce of 71,000 with revenues of $20.6 billion.

However, that's getting ahead of the story we want to tell. In 1989, some 20 years after founding the company, the Rales brothers hired 47-year-old *George Sherman*, then COO of Black & Decker, to become CEO.

During the next ten years, the compounded annual return to shareholders was more than 30%—nearly *twice the rate* of the S&P 500.

Again, not content with sitting back and enjoying the returns, the Rales brothers started looking for Sherman's successor in 1996, just seven years into his reign. This time they found someone from inside the company, 36-year-old *Larry Culp*. After being tested in a series of senior roles, culminating in the post of COO, he finally took over in 2001. Sherman, then 59, retired and left the company.

(*continued*)

(continued)

During the next 14 years, revenues and market capitalisation increased fivefold to nearly $20 billion and $50 billion, respectively. Shareholder returns rose to *five times the rate* of the S&P 500.

But in 2014, Culp, who was still only 51, stepped down and left to become a professor at Harvard Business School. He handed over to another Danaher insider, *Thomas P. Joyce*. "I have some interests outside of the corporate world," Culp said in an interview (citing both fishing and education). "I was doing a lot of soul searching and I was getting ready to go into the 25th year with the company and the 14th year as CEO. I thought that I was ready to move on and the team was ready to carry on in my absence."

Meanwhile, across the Pacific in Japan, another company, clothing chain, *Uniqlo*, was going from strength to strength. Unlike Danaher, it's one of those companies nearly *everyone* has heard of. Tadashi Yanai, the 67-year-old founder (and Chairman, President and CEO) has taken it to a market capitalisation of $30.4 billion and revenues of $14.4 billion (2016 figures). But again, we're getting ahead of our story.

Yanai has two sons, but he's never wanted them to lead the company, even though he believes they have the skills to do so. He prefers them to have an ownership stake of 10% and to be members of the board. He's convinced that operations should be headed by someone who has grown up in the company as a manager: someone who has worked hard for him and yielded results. It wouldn't be fair to bring in an outsider, he claims, and certainly not the founder's sons.

In 2002, after years of explosive growth (and just as Larry Culp was getting into his stride at Danaher), Uniqlo went into a decline. Yanai effectively sacked himself and appointed *Genichi Tamatsuka* from within as President. The new boss had risen through the Uniqlo ranks and done well in the company until then. But over the next few years, business didn't improve. So in 2005 Yanai fired him and returned to operational duties. He's still there. "I think I may not be able to retire," he said in a recent interview. "For me, it's terrible. The biggest part of my job is to quickly develop successors, and around the world I am working to develop new business leaders in the company. But unfortunately, at the moment, there is no one who meets my expectations."

Who is the better CEO—Yanai or Culp? No prizes for the right answer. More importantly, which would *you* rather be?

1.2   A CEO for All Seasons

The moral of the story above is that running a successful business for many years does not necessarily make you a *really* good CEO. You also have to leave a positive legacy.

So where did Yanai go wrong, when it sounded as if he was doing everything right? One explanation is that different circumstances require different kinds of leaders. Diego Bolzonello of Geox (Italy) put it this way: "Different company, different situation. If you're coming from a company that's really strong and successful, and you're going to a company that's in trouble, the approach is totally different." Arguably, it's even harder if you're staying in a company that was once very strong and has fallen on hard times, as poor old Genichi Tamatsuka found to his cost.

In short, it's possible to go from being a stellar leader in one company to an overnight failure in another. As Bob Dudley of BP (UK) warned us, when we sought simple answers from him about CEO success: "There are different types of CEOs with different skill sets. There are 'turn-around CEOs' who stay two to three years, change things and move on." Conversely, there are "stick-around" CEOs, who stay for over a decade. But that doesn't make them irreplaceable or doom the company to disaster when they're gone. The Rales brothers, followed by Sherman and Culp, are proof of that.

There are also geographical variations on the theme of the good CEO. Yang Wansheng of China Machinery Engineering Corporation (China) insisted: "China is different from Western countries. We tried to find good managers through headhunters but the result wasn't that good." In addition, there are different requirements for different industries and different corporate cultures... but we'll have much more to say about that in Class 4.

Vladimir Rashevsky of Suek (Russia) perhaps expressed it best of all, when he told us: "It would be wonderful to have a renaissance man or woman with the complete range of necessary skills and knowledge, but such a person simply does not exist. So, on each occasion you have to try and find the most suitable person for a particular company."

Suffice to say, at this point, generalisations are not always possible when it comes to talking about successful corporate leadership. But that doesn't stop academics making them. So let's take a cursory glance at the history of leadership thought, before we get into practical specifics.

1.3   A Very Brief History of Leadership Theory

It's only in the last few decades that "leadership" has really made it onto the research and teaching agendas of universities and business schools. And there's still surprisingly little focus on the particular role of CEOs.

Nevertheless, philosophising about leadership goes back to Aristotle, Plato and probably even earlier. And theorising about *business* leadership in particular began around the turn of the twentieth century with the work of Max Weber, a German academic, that spanned the fields we now know as economics, sociology, philosophy and law. The earliest theories focused on the idea that a leader is a "great man" or special person "blessed" with unique characteristics, such as charisma, intelligence or motivational gifts. But gradually the emphasis turned, respectively, to character traits, skills, behaviour patterns and, in due course, the relationship between leaders and followers. Today, most leadership experts believe that leaders are made rather than born.

Where today's experts tend to differ from each other is on the question of *how* you make someone into a leader. Some emphasise building cognitive capabilities, such as different types of intelligence (analytical, emotional, social, cultural, etc.). Others focus on developing behavioural skills, such as communication, negotiation, conflict management and the like. A third school of thought (represented by several of our colleagues at INSEAD) argues that becoming a leader is largely about building a "leadership identity." Increasingly, there is an emphasis on "authentic leadership," which means finding the leadership style that suits you, rather than following someone else's recipe for success.

1.4   Our Approach in This Book

For the purposes of this book, we won't espouse any particular school of thought. But we'll start with one insight that all of our "co-authors" and most of our fellow academics agree on. Namely, there can be no such thing as a standard curriculum with a final professional exam for this unique role. Instead, most of the learning required, if you want to become a CEO, has to be gleaned from experience, as you make your steady way to the top.

And, as we've already seen, should you eventually reach the pinnacle and become CEO of a major multinational company, remember that you cannot be considered a great business leader until you have stepped down again. Rather like the ascent of a Himalayan peak, your mission will not be considered a success until you have led your team safely back down again— leaving your people with the ability to scale new heights without you.

In other words, don't expect our *School of CEOs* to be a simple "how to" guide or a step-by-step recipe for success. Rather, it's a well-curated collection of expert insights to apply to your own experiences and leadership development strategies all the way to retirement. After all, the job of CEO is a job like no other. So our *CEO School* was always going to be a school like no other.

SOME FURTHER READING

Bass B. M. (1985). Leadership and performance beyond expectations. New York: Free Press.

Beer M., Eisenstat R. A., Foote N., Fredberg T., Norrgren F. (2011). Higher ambition: How great leaders create economic and social value. Boston, MA: Harvard Business School Press.

Bennis W. G., & Nanus B. (1985). Leaders: Strategies for taking charge. New York: Harper & Row.

Cameron K., Lavine M. (2006). Making the Impossible Possible. San Francisco: Berrett-Koehler Publishers.

Chester B. (1968). The functions of the Executive. Cambridge: Harvard University Press.

Drucker P. (1999). Managing Oneself. Boston: Harvard Business School Publishing.

Drucker P. (1998). Peter Drucker on the Profession of Management. Boston: Harvard Business School Publishing.

Gardner H. (1995). Leading minds. Leading Minds: An Anatomy of Leadership. New York: Basic.

Goleman D. (1995). Emotional Intelligence. New York: Bantam Books.

Katz D., Kahn R. L. (1960). Leadership practices in Relation to Productivity and Morale. In: D. Cartwright and Z. Zander (Eds.) Group Dynamics. Evanston, IL: Harper and Row, 554–570.

Kets de Vries, Manfred F. R. (2006a). The Leadership Mystique: a user's manual for the human enterprise. FT Press.

Kets de Vries, Manfred F. R. (2006b). The Leader on the Couch: A Clinical Approach to Changing People and Organizations. John Wiley & Sons Ltd.

Kets de Vries, Manfred F. R. (2017). Riding the Leadership Rollercoaster. Palgrave Macmillan.

Kotter, J. P. (1988). The leadership factor. New York: Free Press.

Mayo A. J., Nohria N. (2005). In Their Time: The Greatest Business Leaders Of The Twentieth Century. Boston: Harvard Business School Press.

Pfeffer J. (2010). Power: Why Some People Have It and Others Don't. New York: Harper Business.

Podolny J. M., Khurana R., Hill-Popper M. (2005). Revisiting the meaning of leadership. In: Research in Organizational Behavior, Volume 26, 1–36.

Selznick P. (1957). Leadership in Administration. Berkeley, CA: University of California Press.

Tappin S., Cave A. (2010). The New Secrets of CEOs: 200 Global Chief Executives on Leading.

The Best Performing CEOs in the World (2016). Harvard Business Review, November 2016.

Tichy N. M., & Devanna M. A. (1986). The transformational leader: The key to global competitiveness. New York: Wiley.

Wasserman N., Anand B., Nohria N. (2010). When Does Leadership Matter? A Contingent Opportunities View of CEO Leadership. In: R. Khurana, N. Nohria (Eds.) Handbook of Leadership Theory and Practice. Boston: Harvard Business School Press.

Weber M (1964). The Theory of Social and Economic Organization. New York: The Free Press.

CHAPTER 2

Class 2: Personality—The Three Essential Traits of the CEO

Abstract There are three personality traits that our experts believe to be essential for any CEO's success: curiosity, ambition and passion (or CAP for short). Although there's not much talk of curiosity in the academic literature on leadership, for our experts it seems to be a non-negotiable requisite. They also shared some very specific practices that can enhance curiosity—from experimenting to travelling widely and speaking with strangers. Ambition has long been associated with effective leadership, and for our CEOs, the challenge is how to make leadership ambition sustainable. Ironically, according to our interviewees, success can be a bigger threat to ambition than failure. If there's one practical tip that emerges from our research it is: never, ever, rest on your laurels and always keep looking to the future. Passion for what they do helps CEOs to aspire to new heights, learn new tricks, focus on results and enjoy hard work. It's essential for world-class performance in all spheres of human activity—and leadership is no exception.

Keywords Ambition • Curiosity • CEO personality • Passion • Practice • Trait theories of leadership

> *A chi vuole, non mancano modi. (Italy)*
> *Meaning: Where there is a will, there is a way. (If you are determined enough, then you'll achieve what you wish.)*

Nothing ventured, nothing gained (UK)

Those who lose dreaming are lost. (Indigenous Australian)

해안이 보이지 않는 것을 이겨낼 용기가 없다면 절대로 바다를 건널 수
(Korea)
   Meaning: You can never cross the ocean until you have the courage to lose sight of the shore.

"I don't believe that people are born as CEOs. Anybody can train, improve, learn," asserts Temel Kotil of Turkish Airlines. Richard Rushton of Distell (South Africa) agrees: "There's no formula for the kind of personality that makes for successful CEOs." So does Peter J. Coleman of Woodside (Australia), who claims: "If a CEO is an introvert or an extrovert it doesn't matter."

Yet, having spoken at length to these 3 CEOs and 17 others, we're not sure things are quite that simple. Admittedly, there's no Myers-Briggs-type personality test, no interpretation of a psychologist's inkblot, no Harry-Potter-style "sorting hat" that will magically separate potential CEOs from the rest of humanity. But based on our 20 conversations, we believe there are certain personality traits that the *majority* of good CEOs share.

Before sharing our findings, as we're curious types, we have a couple of questions for you:

1. Imagine you're having a busy day at work. Someone new has just joined your department, and a colleague brings them round to meet everyone. Do you:

   (a) Look up from your computer, smile, say "hello"... and get straight back to your long to-do list?
   (b) Briefly introduce yourself, explain your role and say you'll be happy to provide help or advice, once you're less busy?
   (c) Briefly introduce yourself and your job, offer further help at a later date... then spend five minutes finding out all about your new workmate?

(*continued*)

(continued)

2. Now you're back home after your busy day—and totally exhausted. You have flopped down in front of the television and are flicking through the channels looking for an easy watch, when you come across a breaking news report about a major technological breakthrough. Do you:

(a) Move on as fast as you can in search of a comedy or an action film?

(b) Linger on the news item long enough to get the gist, before returning to your quest for some real entertainment?

(c) Watch the entire report and then head for the Internet or a 24-hour news channel to find out as much as you possibly can?

If you answered (c) both times, then you're probably a curious type too—just like us and our 20 CEOs. In fact, curiosity is the one must-have character trait that almost all of them mentioned to us in some way or another.

2.1   PERSONALITY TRAIT 1: CURIOSITY—CURIOUSER AND CURIOUSER?

Although there isn't much talk of curiosity in the academic literature on leadership, we're not the first to highlight its importance. Jeff Immelt of General Electric (USA) has noticed the prevalence of inquisitiveness in the elite business-leading population too. "The CEOs I know are unbelievably curious, and they have that constant thirst for information, for knowledge, for learning," he told us. "I think this is a number one attribute of every successful person I've ever met—from Mark Zuckerberg to Steve Jobs and Warren Buffett. They have this incredible curiosity about world change and what's going on."

And Vladimir Rashevsky of SUEK (Russia) sums up our first finding in five words: "You *have to* be inquisitive."

But what does that mean exactly? Peter Coleman has the answer. "An inquisitive mind is willing to accept and explore different ways of doing things," he says. In other words, curiosity is basically what makes people seek new experiences and challenge their own assumptions.

But that's only one way among many of putting it. In fact, we heard about curiosity so many times during our interviews that we almost lost count. We'll content ourselves with passing on just five insights from five of our co-authors, each suggesting a way in which curiosity can play a bigger role in anyone's professional life. We call them curiosity-enhancing practices, and we believe they are also performance-enhancing practices for all knowledge workers, CEOs included.

1. **Experimenting—at work (or at the weekend).** Bob Dudley of BP (UK) told us about his baptism of fire following the merger of BP and Amoco in 1998: "After the deal I was thrown into China. I knew very little and had no one to consult. (CEOs are very lonely most of the time, you know!) So I went along by trying different things and reflecting on the outcomes. In Russia (as the CEO of a joint venture TNK-BP) I often found myself in similar situations. You learn by trial and error."

   It's tempting to think that, if you really want to be successful, you should be careful not to make too many errors (we'll have more to say about this in Class 4). But there are some comparatively risk-free parts of most jobs where making mistakes matters less than others. And, failing that, you can always develop your curiosity by experimenting outside of work: tasting new cuisines, trying new sports or reading a different newspaper.

2. **Challenging your thinking.** Temel Kotil says of himself and other CEOs he knows: "There's a need to challenge—challenge yourself, challenge everybody, challenge everything." Or, to put it another way, it's important not to get stuck in an intellectual and professional rut.

   Again, this is an observation to handle with care. Challenging the status quo is something that goes down better in certain contexts and cultures than others. Some bosses like to be questioned and are suspicious of people who always agree with them. Others don't like to be doubted. And sometimes there's a good reason for doing things the way they've always been done. You have to gauge the circumstances and personalities involved, clearly. But by putting carefully judged questions to the right person at the right time, you can flex your curiosity muscles.

3. **Travelling widely and talking to new people.** Richard Rushton says: "CEOs need to travel, need to discover, need to have an inquiring mind, need to meet people socially outside of work, particularly in a globally interconnected, changing world."

   As Rushton suggests, there's no need for an executive expense account or an expat assignment to explore other cultures. One of the great benefits of today's "globally interconnected" world is that there are probably plenty of people from different cultures or social groups to encounter in your own neighbourhood.

4. **Getting out of your comfort zone.** Nishi Vasudeva of Hindustan Petroleum Corporation (India) reflects that young professionals often lack the confidence to accept responsibilities beyond their own area of expertise. She says: "Stepping out of the comfort zone will take you somewhere completely different. That's where the individual shows up. Opportunities given by your company are one thing, but the individual has to say: *Yes, I will take that job and improve myself.*"

   Remember, no one's going to offer you a job that they don't think you could do; so if you get an offer to work in a department or function you know nothing about, seize your chance with both hands and treat it as an opportunity to learn… rather than a test of how to hide your ignorance.

5. **Reading books you don't *have* to read for your professional development.** Lee Chul Kyoon (Korea, Daelim) believes: "Reading books is the most important thing to develop yourself." His reasoning for this is quite practical. "While we're working," he says, "we don't have much time."

   But we'd go one step further. Reading books allows you to see the world through other people's eyes, to travel without going places—even to go back in time. In fact, most of the CEOs we met don't just read books about how to be a good leader. Many of them read about history, politics, other industries, other cultures… even novels. For those who are feeling particularly curious, here's a reading list compiled from our interviews.

A Reading List for Future CEOs

Jeff Immelt (USA, General Electric): "I'm a big reader of *military history*. Gettysburg is my favorite historical battle of the American Civil War, because it was all about mistakes. The side that won was the side that made the fewest mistakes. But they all still made mistakes. And then I tend to read *technical journals...* about the aviation industry, oil and gas, energy. These are my two major sources of development!"

Mazen Ahmed Khayyat (Saudi Arabia, El Khayyat): "I regularly read books *on team building, management of teams and leading the board*. I believe these are essential, especially in multi-business-unit companies."

Diego Bolzonello (Italy, Geox): "Read, read. Keep understanding the world. *I don't have time to go to conferences, but I read the reports.* I'm a guy who prefers to inform myself."

Shuzo Kaihori (Japan, Yokogawa): "I was just reading the analyses of the nuclear incident at Fukushima. Also I read about *different cultures*: comparisons of Japanese culture to Western culture. Sometimes I also read Japanese *novels*."

Richard Rushton (South Africa, Distell): "I read anything from Bloomberg to politics in the US, the current Syria situation, what's happening in the Chinese real estate market, as well as the issues that South Africa faces with its own political and economic dynamics. *A CEO needs to be a reader, a quick reader of events: geopolitical, social and otherwise*."

We believe an inquisitive nature is necessary, not just desirable—a non-negotiable requisite for any candidate for the top job. Indeed, it seems that *not* being curious can be a downright danger. Constantino Galanis of Química Apollo (Mexico) told us: "The biggest mistake is that certain people think they know everything. Basically, a CEO must be alert with eyes wide open all the time."

Perhaps too, being curious is not so far from being *humble*, as Renato Bertani (Brazil, Barra Energia) suggests: "I still rank being humble—and understanding that you don't know everything—as a key quality that any leader would have to have." Or, as Richard Rushton puts it, "The very big danger with long-serving CEOs is that they start to believe their own stories—and that's dangerous in a changing world."

Humility isn't necessarily a personality trait that's normally associated with CEOs, but then, our research for this book threw up a lot of surprises.

At this point in the class, let's take a break for another quick personality test:

---

3. Imagine (or remember) yourself aged 18 or thereabouts... You're contemplating your future and applying to college or university, and you're lucky enough not to have any significant financial constraints. Do you:

(a) Apply to the most local institutions you can find—even if they don't have a brilliant reputation—so that you can live at home and see your friends every weekend?

(b) Apply to institutions with a better reputation, even if they're a long way from home—but only those you're fairly certain you can get into? Why risk disappointment?

(c) Apply to the very best institutions that you have some chance of getting into, regardless of where they are in the country—or even the world?

4. Now imagine (or remember) yourself aged 65 or thereabouts. You're about to retire, after a hugely successful career. How do you plan to spend your newfound free time?

(a) On the golf course/by the pool/in the garden/with family and friends/with a good book/on a cruise ship (delete or add alternative leisure activities as applicable).

(b) Enjoying yourself, of course, and doing just enough light consultancy or non-exec work not to get bored.

(c) What free time? You've already got several board memberships, volunteer activities and even a few entrepreneurial or investment ventures lined up. And then there's that book you're planning to write... or the PhD you never got around to doing.

If you continued to answer mainly (c), then you're most likely not only curious but ambitious. Congratulations! You have the second personality trait required to become an effective CEO.

2.2   PERSONALITY TRAIT 2: AMBITION—REACH FOR THE STARS?

Perhaps it's fairly obvious that CEOs need to be ambitious. To get to the top, you have to want to get there. And this attitude isn't exactly rare, as Abdel F. Badwi of Bankers Petroleum (Canada) points out: "People who do an MBA at a top school usually have an ambition to be a CEO. Perhaps even half of bachelor students [undergraduates] are people who have a desire to be a CEO."

But desire certainly isn't enough—or that top MBA school. You also need deep-rooted ambition. "For me," says Richard Rushton, "successful CEOs demonstrate success, ambition and seeing things through to a logical conclusion. That's not determined by the quality of the school, but your own drive."

In other words, you don't just need a desire to succeed but the determination to keep on succeeding. Shuzo Kaihori of Yokogawa (Japan) puts it nicely: "We have to be always with fresh eyes, not relying on past successes."

More problematically, you also have to believe in yourself, when others don't. Only ambition can bring down the barriers that bias puts up. It's a sad fact, for instance, that women need more ambition than men to break through the proverbial glass ceiling. One of the most powerful personal examples of ambition that we encountered on our G20 journey was the only woman: Nishi Vasudeva.[1] Her story reveals just how much more ambition women need, compared to their male counterparts. "There were times when I had to pack my kids off to another city to my mother," she recalls. "I just managed. What I'm saying is that, if you want to do as well as men, then do whatever it takes."

This is not to say that men can't be victims of bias as well. "When you look at my history," says Stefan Messer of Messer Group (Germany), "nobody thought that I could be the CEO of the company." This is often the case in a family business, where there can sometimes be prejudice against family members (while other family firms may have the opposite bias and be reluctant to appoint non-family CEOs!). Or maybe the company simply had a traditional preference for a professional engineers, rather than commercial experts. Either way, only ambition and determination kept Stefan Messer going through the dark years when the company was taken over by outsiders who took it to the brink of oblivion (as we'll hear in Class 4).

[1] And before you accuse *us* of gender bias in our selection of CEOs, take note of the statistics. In Europe and the USA, only around 3–4% of CEO's of large publicly listed companies are women. And it's worse in other parts of the world. So we're doing well to have achieved 5% in our sample.

Ironically, it seems, success can be a bigger threat to ambition than failure of the kind that Messer Group experienced. If there's one practical insight that emerges from our interviews it's this: *never, ever, rest on your laurels and always keep looking to the future.* As Richard Rushton says, "The reason there's no qualification that grants you the right to become CEO is that qualifications only assess your ability based on the past." "I think the way to groom a CEO," agrees Renato Bertani, "is to keep professionals challenged, to give them constant challenges, and the tools to meet challenging targets." In other words, perhaps ambition can be honed through training.

Before we take another break for a few questions, we'll leave you with some more of Jeff Immelt's words of wisdom: "I see some of my peers and they think that the day they became CEO was the best of their life. It's their crowning achievement. But I thought it was the first day of my life when I became CEO of GE… like I was a baby again."

This comment illustrates the crucial difference between "ambition" in the sense of an all-pervading personality trait and "*an* ambition" in the sense of a single objective—like making a million dollars, buying a Ferrari or becoming the boss. Truly ambitious characters, like Immelt and our other interviewees, always want to go one step further. Achieving their goals is never enough.

To distract you from your ambitions for a moment, here's one last personality test:

This time, give yourself a point every time you answer "yes":

1. When you're faced with a task, do you always give it 100%?
2. Do you sometimes get so absorbed in what you're doing that you lose all track of time?
3. Do you often push yourself to your limit?
4. Is your enthusiasm sometimes infectious?
5. When you've got something you need to work on, do you find you can't relax?
6. Do you get excited about the things you like to do?
7. Do you talk to people about the stuff you enjoy in life?
8. Do you try to involve people in your favourite activities?
9. Think about your favourite food or film. Obviously you like it, but do you absolutely *love* it?
10. When you try a new activity, do you immerse yourself in it completely (as opposed to just dipping your toe in the water)?

If you scored 7 or higher, then you're almost certainly a passionate kind of person… which, you'll be pleased to know, is another frequently found feature of CEOs.

2.3   PERSONALITY TRAIT 3: PASSION—THE BIG PARADOX?

It was with a slightly confessional tone that Temel Kotil told us: "The potential CEO should be integrated by heart with the company—be 100% committed, love the company more than anything else (just leave my son and daughters out that!)—and love it more than anybody else, including all the employees, stakeholders and investors, even the owners."

"I don't know how common my behaviour is," he added.

Well, after 19 other interviews, we can confirm that his behaviour is indeed the norm, rather than an exception. Again, it seems to be one of those non-negotiable prerequisites of having the corner office on the top floor. Passion wasn't something that all of the CEOs in our sample talked about by any means. But it's something we saw, heard or felt in the presence of each and every one of them. Their eyes lit up, or they became animated when they spoke about their companies or industries. They came up with stories and ideas spontaneously. They *enthused*. Don't assume that you have to be an extrovert to show passion, either. This isn't a personality trait confined to a certain Myers-Briggs (or any other psychological model's) category.

Some of our interviewees did refer directly to passion. And here's what they had to say.

Don't Ration Your Passion!
Abdel F. Badwi: "I always try to be passionate about what I'm trying to accomplish—and passionate about the vision for the company."

Diego Bolzonello (Italy, Geox): "Never say 'I don't care'. The CEO always cares."

Jean Sentenac (France, Axens): "For me, a CEO first of all has to have a spirit for the good of the company in the short and long term. This person will place the company above everything else in his or her life. I always think first about the company. Of course, a family life is very important to me and a source of stability, but

(continued)

(continued)

the interests of my company dictate my decisions and my behaviour outside of it."

Jeffrey Immelt: "There's not a minute during the day that I don't think about the company. There's not an interaction that I don't put in a company context. So, I think it's a love. It's a passion. And it's my inspiration. I'm not weird or anything! I'm a happily married man with a nice family. It's just my complete passion."

Some people might say that "managing your passion" or even "managing *with* passion" are contradictions in terms. But José Ángel Sánchez of Real Madrid (Spain) isn't one of them. The general manager of one of the world's greatest soccer clubs, he claims that "football is all about passion"—and that it was the same in his former industry of computer gaming. "Everything is pure emotion around a football club or games company," he says. What's more, he insists, "The lesson from football is that passion is something you can manage."

So how do you go about managing passion? More specifically, how can you develop more of it? There's a fundamental paradox about passion, it seems the more you spend, the more you have. Richard Rushton, for example, describes the way his hobbies feed into his enthusiasm for his work. "Without them," he says, "I don't think I'd be able to save enough energy of passion." In short, he suggests that passion defies the laws of conservation of energy. Activities outside the office, whether family days out or gruelling sessions on the sports pitch, don't exhaust your supply of enthusiasm but instead regenerate you for the challenges of the working week.

We'll have more to say about this in Class 7. For now, however, we'll content ourselves with one final (if somewhat obvious) remark: no one can develop a passion for a job, an organisation or an industry they don't feel positively about. Passion may defy the laws of physics, but it can't be conjured out of thin air.

2.4   CAP Stands for Curiosity, Ambition, Passion

Let's recap. Or maybe reCAP. So far, in Class 2, we've covered the three personality characteristics—identified by our sample of CEOs—that we believe nearly all successful business leaders have in spadefuls: curiosity, ambition, passion—or CAP for short.

You won't find much about curiosity, ambition or passion in the traditional leadership textbooks. Nor is CAP on the syllabus in management schools. Maybe it's because these are traits you're born with—and can't teach or develop… or can you?

Think about it. Human beings are almost by definition curious, ambitious and passionate. If we weren't curious, we'd never learn to talk or to use the word "why," as all toddlers do. If we weren't ambitious, we'd never teach ourselves to walk or ride a bicycle. If we weren't passionate, we'd never scream to be fed or have tantrums. We all develop these characteristics before we go to school. And then, somewhere along the line of our education, most of us lose them.

Now, that's not entirely a bad thing. Unbridled CAP can have its dangers. "Curiosity killed the cat," as the old saying goes, while blind ambition plunged Lady Macbeth into a Shakespearean bloodbath. And the very fact that many of the world's legal systems are so lenient about "crimes of passion" just tells us where obsessional feelings can take us. Clearly you need to control your CAP to lead a healthy, normal life.

But, we promise, our *School of CEOs* is one educational establishment that's not going to beat the CAP out of you. In fact, the ideas in Class 2 can help you to maximise your CAP quotient, by building on your natural human tendencies to be curious, ambitious and passionate—alongside whatever other personality traits you happen to have.

So, even if you didn't pass our personality tests with flying colours, don't despair. You can improve your CAP quotient, by heeding the insights from our CEOs in Class 2. You may be highly curious and passionate but need to work on your ambition. Or you might be extremely ambitious but lacking curiosity and passion (like some of the MBA students we encounter). Everyone is different. But everyone can be more curious, ambitious and passionate.

There's an old proverb: "If the cap fits, wear it." Well, we say, wear the CAP, even if it doesn't fit you yet. This won't be enough on its own to take you to the top and succeed as a CEO. CAP is necessary but not sufficient, as the mathematics textbooks say. That's why you also need to read Classes 3 to 8.…

SOME FURTHER READING

Bass, B. M. (1985) Leadership and Performance Beyond Expectations. New York; Free Press.

Bennis, W., Spreitzer, G. M. (2001) The Future of leadership. Today's top leadership thinkers speak to tomorrow's leaders. San Francisco: Jossey-Bass Inc.

Drucker, P. F. (1954) The Practice of Management. New York: Harper and Row.

Drucker, P. (1999) Managing Oneself. Boston: Harvard Business School Publishing.

Goleman, D., Boyatzis, R. and McKee, A. (2002) Primal Leadership: Realizing the Power of Emotional Intelligence. Boston: Harvard Business School.

Johansen, B. (2009) Leaders Make the Future. Ten New Leadership Skills for an Uncertain World. San Francisco: Berrett-Koehler Publishers, Inc.

Kets de Vries, M. F. R. (2006a). The Leadership Mystique: a user's manual for the human enterprise. FT Press.

Kets de Vries, M. F. R. (2006b). The Leader on the Couch: A Clinical Approach to Changing People and Organizations. John Wiley & Sons Ltd.

Kets de Vries, M. F. R. (2017). Riding the Leadership Rollercoaster. Palgrave Macmillan.

Krames, J. A. (2002) The Jack Welch Lexicon of Leadership. New York: McGraw-Hill.

Reeves, M., Harnoss, J. An Agenda for the Future of Global Business. Harvard Business Review, 2017. https://hbr.org/2017/02/an-agenda-for-the-future-of-global-business

Shakespeare, W. (2015). Macbeth. New York: Diversion Books.

Staogdill, R. M. (1974) Handbook of Leadership: A Survey of the Literature. New York: The Free Press.

Useem, M (1998) The Leadership Moment. New York: Three Rivers Book.

Velsor E.V., McCauley C.D., Ruderman M.N. (Eds.) (2010) The Center for Creative Leadership Handbook of Leadership Development. Third Edition. San Francisco: Jossey-Bass.

CHAPTER 3

Class 3: Education—Three Academic Proverbs for Future CEOs

Abstract Engineering or economics? Science or humanities? Bachelor of Commerce or top-ranked MBA? Is formal education essential for an effective CEO of the twenty-first century? The answer is more complex than you might expect. Both our experts and quantitative research suggest there is little correlation between area of study and CEO performance. Attending a high-ranked business school helps people to advance faster to the top job and get higher pay, but it doesn't guarantee superior results.

What our experts agree on—and we second them—is the critical role of formal education in developing such fundamentals for today's business leaders' abilities as analytical, critical and systemic thinking ("the CEO mindset") and lifelong learning capacity. Diego Bolzonello (CEO of Geox, Italy) puts it this way: "School means training to understand."

For future CEOs most lifelong learning will take place outside the classroom. However, never underestimate the crucial role played by formal education in teaching you to get the most out of your real-world experience. And if you didn't have the good fortune to acquire your learning in a university lecture theatre, you can still catch up… but you will have to work a lot harder.

Keywords Education • Formal business education • MBA programme • Lifelong learning • University

© The Author(s) 2018
S. Shekshnia et al., *CEO School*,
https://doi.org/10.1007/978-981-10-7865-1_3

師傅領進門, 修行在個人 *(China)*
Meaning: Teachers open the door. You enter by yourself. (English equivalent:
You can lead the horse to the water, but you can't make it drink.)

Nadie escarmienta en cabeza ajena. (Mexico)
Meaning: Nobody learns in the head of someone else. (That is, you have to
make your own mistakes.)

Engineering or economics? Science or humanities? Bachelor of Commerce
or top-ranked MBA? Or perhaps you don't need any kind of higher education to become a CEO. Is the University of Life (and Work) enough?

The simple, two-letter answer would seem to be "no." All of our 20
co-authors—without exception—attended university or some other kind
of higher education institution (as did we). Admittedly, this is a pretty
small sample. But go to any major company website and click through to
the executive team bios—and you'll find that nearly all of them mention a
degree programme. Sometimes the face smiling out at you from the cheesy
corporate head-and-shoulders pic will be well into his sixties or seventies.
It hardly seems relevant what he studied or which institution he attended
more than four decades ago... but somehow it matters. Why?

3.1   What Is It About Education?

"I believe leadership starts at the education level. It starts to be built at the
school level and then progresses into university," says Abdel F. Badwi of
Bankers Petroleum (Canada). But he has a degree in geology, which
doesn't sound the most obvious form of training for the highest strata of
management.

Stefan Messer of Messer Group (Germany) is the only member of our
CEO cohort, who appears to take issue with the importance of higher
education: "CEO is not a profession you can learn at university: practical
experience is much more important than theoretical education," he says.
But he is hardly a self-taught man himself. He has a degree in economics.
Messer, like so many other family business leaders, didn't go straight into
the family firm from high school, even though it was presumably an option
for him. He—or at least his parents—must have believed there was a value
in university-level study.

Perhaps it's time to leave opinions aside and seek out some rigorous
research. It turns out that there's plenty of it....

Some Interesting Research Projects and Their Findings

- Margaret Lindorff and Elizabeth Prior Jonson of Monash University in Melbourne looked at the relationship between the performance of Australia's top 200 companies and the business education of their CEOs. They found *absolutely no correlation* between the CEO having a business degree and either three-year or five-year return to shareholders.
- Sanjai Bhagat, Brian Bolton and Ajay Subramanian (Universities of Colorado at Boulder, New Hampshire and Georgia State, respectively) analysed a massive sample of the USA's largest 1,500 firms. They concluded there was some evidence that having a CEO with an MBA from a top-20 business school was associated with a high-performing business but that this was statistically weak. However, they discovered that—even when the previous CEO was fired—*companies tended to hire a replacement with the same kind of educational background.*
- Aron A. Gottesman and Matthew R. Morey of Pace University, New York, compared the performances of companies led by CEOs from elite educational backgrounds with those who had attended less prestigious institutions and/or who had attained lower levels of qualifications. Surprise, surprise, *those with top schools on their CVs got slightly worse business results than the lower educational achievers... but significantly higher compensation!*
- Vincent L. Barker and George C. Mueller (University of Kansas, Lawrence, and University of Milwaukee, Wisconsin, respectively) found that *companies where the CEO had a technical degree tended to spend more on R&D*, which might (possibly) lead to better performance.

Everything points to the same conclusion. The research backs up our small samples, web searches, CEO opinions and most responsible parents' advice. There is simply no evidence of correlation—let alone causal effect—between the performance of a company and the quality (or subject specialism) of its CEO's education. Yet the fact is that 99.9% of CEOs have a university-level degree.

Okay, we know there are a few celebrated exceptions. They're so famous that you're probably already listing them in your head. Steve Jobs and Michael Dell were college dropouts, and Richard Branson, who is notoriously dyslexic, never got there in the first place. And then there's Bill Gates or more recently Mark Zuckerberg (although it was Harvard that they both dropped out of, which already makes them better educated than over 7 billion other human beings).

Note, however, that all of these famous exceptions are founder-entrepreneurs. If they hadn't created hugely successful companies, they probably wouldn't have been appointed to lead them. And indeed, while Dell and Zuckerberg are still in post, Jobs, Gates and Branson were all replaced by highly qualified graduates.

Yes, even companies founded by non-graduates go on to appoint people with good degrees as successor CEOs—with a preference for candidates who attended elite universities or attained good grades elsewhere. And they persist in this course of action, even though there isn't a shred of evidence to prove it right. So what's going on?

The uncharitable explanation is that most of those responsible for appointing CEOs of big companies themselves had elite-level educations—and they are naturally biased towards selecting candidates in their own image.

But we have a more charitable hypothesis, which is that the members of CEO selection panels are well aware of what they gained from their education. They know from their own experience that highly educated people are more able to find and process information—and are more adaptive to change—than those who didn't get a degree.

In other words a university-level education trains people to think in a way that's very useful to CEOs. Or as Diego Bolzonello of Geox (Italy) summed it up, when we met him, "Analysis is very important and that you get from school."

The fact is, the more VUCA (volatile, uncertain, complex and ambiguous) our world gets, the more important the ability to find information, to make sense of it and to take a non-standard decision becomes. And there's nothing quite like formal education for developing this ability. Rather than blindly following management formulae, CEOs need to be able to calculate from first principles when small changes add up to trends, where uncertainties constitute risks, how simplicity can be conjured out of complexity and which side of ambiguity the truth falls. Instinct born of long experience or entrepreneurial self-belief is no longer sufficient for good business judgement.

Hence the first of our three conclusions of this chapter, which we'll present in the form of our own homemade proverbs.

Proverb 1: It's analysis that prevents paralysis.

We all know, there's a phenomenon known as "analysis paralysis": over-thinking a decision to the point that it never gets made. But the alternative is worse—at least in today's turbulent environment. A decision without analysis is just a roll of the dice: a matter of luck. And in a highly complex world, the odds of a random judgement turning out to be the right one are vanishingly low. It's the ability to select information, analyse it properly and make a decision that saves CEOs and their companies from getting stuck, like rabbits in the headlights, in the fast lane of twenty-first-century business.

The beauty of university-level learning is that there's never any opportunity for analysis paralysis. The essays, assignments, problem sheets and exams fly at you so fast that there's no time to sit around over-thinking your conclusions (even though, paradoxically, there's plenty of time to sit around drinking a lot of coffee and having intense conversations about the meaning of life, long into the night).

3.2   A Degree Is More Than an Education

Learning the gift of analysis isn't the only benefit of studying for a degree, though. Higher education is also a way to leave home, to travel, to stand on your own two feet, to find a paid job, to make lifelong contacts. As the personal story below hints, there's something about student life that mirrors the entrepreneurial process or even the pioneer experience that turns so many immigrants into successful business people. For young people from well-off backgrounds, it can be the first time they experience hardship. And that's a thoroughly good thing, if they want to cultivate some of the ambition and passion we covered in Class 2. In other words, university or business school is much more than a place of formal education. It's a way to build character.

An Oilman's Story: Miguel Galuccio (YPF, Argentina)
I come from the countryside in Argentina, from an ordinary family. My father was a middle-class entrepreneur with many small businesses. There are lots of people like this in Argentina. Perhaps it's because we are a country of immigrants—like my grandfather, who came from Italy when he was 14. Those are people who practically had nothing. I left the countryside for Buenos Aires, because that's where the best schools are, and entered the best engineering school in Argentina. I worked to pay for my university studies, as they were private. When I finished, I decided to go abroad to make a career.

In addition, to reliving his grandfather's immigrant experience, Miguel Galuccio clearly got his career off to a flying start by studying at a top engineering school. So did several of our other CEOs. Some of them even added a top MBA school to their CVs. And a couple have PhDs. "Intellectual capabilities are important," says Temel Kotil of Turkish Airlines (Turkey), who was a professor of aeronautics before going into the airline industry.

We can't help agreeing with him. After all, all three of us were educated to doctoral level, and two of us have taught at a range of leading business schools. We believe in education. On the other hand, two of us have been CEOs, which—alas—proved conclusively that intellectual prowess was of limited use in business leadership. Likewise for our attendance of prestigious schools.

As Richard Rushton of Distell (South Africa) says, "I believe there's no relevance whatsoever in the fact that an individual went to a top school or a bottom school. I think the fact that they applied themselves in whatever school they attended is important, as successful CEOs must be able to see things through to a logical conclusion. Top schools clearly have an advantage in that they attract top people, and it's not a bad thing to have been to one. But the person and their attributes are the ultimate qualifier."

Here then, is our second proverb.

> **Proverb 2: Being a high flyer doesn't help you *climb* to the top.**

Be that as it may, there's one type of higher degree that most budding CEOs aim to add to their résumé—and that's the MBA (which stands for "Master of Business Administration" not, as the old joke goes, "Mediocre But Arrogant"). As MBA programmes have become more and more fashionable, so they've filtered into the résumés of star CEOs like Jeffrey Immelt of General Electric (USA), who has famously been with GE since getting his MBA from Harvard Business School—after graduating in applied mathematics and economics from Dartmouth College, another Ivy League school.

In an interview with CNBC (quoted by online resource Poets and Quants), Immelt confided: "Business school is one of the most intense times of your life. There are times you feel overwhelmed from the standpoint that it's midnight, I have another case to read, I don't really understand the subject material, and you say: 'Gosh, what am I going to do?'"

Immelt seems to be saying that business school gave him the opportunity to repeat the too-much-to-do-in-too-little-time experience of higher education that we mentioned earlier—but with even more intensity and even less opportunity for analysis paralysis.

Surely, though, it must be more than that—or MBA programmes wouldn't cost so much more than other master's-level degrees! And indeed, there *is* some statistical evidence for the value of an MBA. When our INSEAD colleagues, Herminia Ibarra, Urs Peyer and Morten Hansen compiled a ranking of the "Best-Performing CEOs in the World" for *Harvard Business Review* in 2010, they discovered that bosses with MBAs were positioned, on average, 40 places higher than those without. Although there's no suggestion that the majority of these went to one of the "Best-Performing Business Schools in the World," it seems a significant finding.

What proportion of the top-performing CEOs actually have MBAs? *Harvard Business Review* has continued using more or less the same methodology—based on shareholder return across a CEO's entire tenure—every year since our colleagues first compiled their ranking. And each time the new top 100 is published, around a quarter of the list are holders of MBA degrees. The percentage is about the same in our small, handpicked sample of 20. Among current Fortune 500 CEOs (see pie chart below), the proportion is much higher at 42%—although 121 out of the 500 didn't go to any kind of graduate school (Fig. 3.1).

**What kind of degrees do
Fortune 500 CEOs have?**

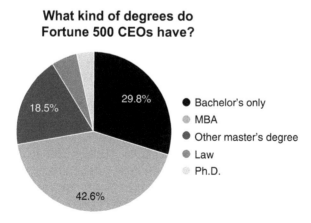

Fig. 3.1   Educational qualifications of Fortune 500 CEOs

The conclusion is obvious: an MBA is not a necessity for CEO success. But equally clearly, it helps.

Increasingly too, we're seeing a new breed of entrepreneurs emerging from MBA classrooms: ambitious young graduates who decide to become a CEO of a large company by building one. Elon Musk, who gained an MBA from Wharton, springs to mind, as do some of our own former students. We're proud to have among them Michel de Rovira, INSEAD MBA 2007, who with his partner built Michel et Augustin into a global food brand and multi-million-euro business, and Gleb Frank, INSEAD MBA 2011, the CEO of a large private equity company. It's as if an MBA is a kind of incubator that gives you a year (or two) to build your business plan, feeding in everything you learn in real time.

But the fact remains that most CEOs don't start out as entrepreneurs. So, what is it about an MBA that accelerates people up the career ladder to the corner office?

Our hunch is that an MBA is perhaps more a symptom than a cause of CEO success. It's a degree designed to attract the ambitious and curious (remember those all-important traits from Class 2?). People go to business school to get a CV-boost and a network, as well as to gain knowledge. We're not sure whether passion (the third all-important trait from Class 2) comes into the equation, but—as Meatloaf (also a college graduate) famously sang—"two out of three ain't bad."

More importantly, perhaps, the MBA is a degree designed for people with a *certain kind* of curiosity. They're once specialists who are now in search of breadth. At least, that's what Nishi Vasudeva (Hindustan Petroleum Corporation, India) seems to put her finger on, as she reflects on her own success story.

An Oilwoman's Story: Nishi Vasudeva (Hindustan Petroleum Corporation, India)
You need to have a fair enough understanding of most parts of the business... In our industry, most people who join are engineers, because it is a technical field. But I graduated in economics and after that I went to the Indian Institute of Management in Calcutta, which is one of our premier schools, for my MBA. To be able to do a good job at the top it is important that you are exposed to different areas. If you just grow in one area, you will become a real expert, but your experience—and understanding—of others isn't there.

3.3   SUBJECT MATTERS?

Note that Nishi Vasudeva is at pains to point out she's not an engineer. And others from similarly technical businesses agree that an engineering degree is not a necessity to reach the top of the tree. Stefan Messer (Messer Group, Germany)—who happens to be an economics graduate at the helm of an industrial gases company—says, "There's no need for a special education to be a CEO. You can be a lawyer, you can be a salesman, you can be a technician."

However, the facts don't necessarily align with these particular opinions. Returning to the *Harvard Business Review* ranking of the "Best-Performing CEOs in the World," around 25% of the 2016 top 100 were engineering graduates. That's as many as had MBAs. And the numbers in our small sample of 20 are even more striking. Around half of our CEO co-authors studied engineering of some kind at university (see Fig. 3.2).

Nevertheless, these numbers don't necessarily convince the engineers themselves that an engineering degree is so important for those aspiring to CEO status. "Myself, I am an engineer," says Jean Sentenac of Axens (France). "But you have many successful companies where the CEOs came from a financial background and they have been quite successful also." Another engineer by training, Shuzo Kaihori of Yokogawa Electric Corporation (Japan), agrees. "Technical or economic, it doesn't matter," he says.

**What first-degree discipline do our 20
CEOs come from?**

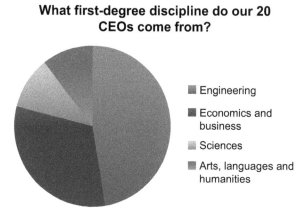

- Engineering
- Economics and business
- Sciences
- Arts, languages and humanities

Fig. 3.2   Degree disciplines of our 20 CEOs

Constantino Galanis of Química Apollo (Mexico) is equally adamant. "Education is the most important thing—as much education someone can get and digest—as an engineer, lawyer, businessman." And he has both an engineering degree and an MBA... so who are we to disagree?

Funnily enough, it takes a philosopher to point out that different specialisations bring different benefits—and that choice of degree subject may be culturally determined anyway.

A Philosopher's Story: José Ángel Sánchez (Real Madrid, Spain)
I am not a typical CEO who has a good track record of academics. My path has been totally different. I have a degree in philosophy. I am a humanist, not an engineer. This gave me a certain ability to watch: to read between lines and understand the importance of relationships. I read that this profile was now very popular in certain companies in the States and Japan—people who studied history or philosophy. In my opinion, if you have a technical education, this human information from subjects like philosophy should be learned later. It's something basic, something we all should have.

Taking José Ángel Sánchez's advice, we went back and read between the lines of this chapter to reach the third of our proverbial conclusions.

Proverb 3: It's not *what* you learn that counts. It's learning *how* to learn that matters.

The only one of our interviewees to say this explicitly (if in different words) was Diego Bolzonello of Geox (Italy). "School means training to understand," he told us. "If you understand a book, you understand a lesson, you understand a teacher, it means that you are trained to understand. It's very important."

The more we think about his words, the more they make sense. At high school you learn. At university, engineering institute or business school you carry on learning. But there, something else happens: you become responsible for your own learning. That is, you learn *how* to learn. Ultimately, it doesn't matter what subject you choose to study or how well you do in your exams, as long as you take the opportunity to channel the curiosity, ambition and passion we saw in Class 2 into a lifelong ability and desire to learn.

It goes without saying that most of the lifelong learning any of us acquire will take place outside the classroom. As Miguel Galuccio (YPF, Argentina) puts it, "Becoming a CEO is not about academic qualifications. I believe it is a matter of being tested on your corporate ladder, step by step."

However, never underestimate the crucial role played by formal education in teaching you to get the most out of your real-world experience. And certainly don't underestimate the power of a prestigious education to get you onto the shortlist for a senior job.

Now that you've understood that, we can leave behind the cosier classrooms of our CEO School and get out into the field. Our next class will be about building the right portfolio of early career experience to become a good CEO. Welcome to the School of Hard Knocks.

Some Further Reading

Barker, V. L. & Mueller, G. C. (2002) CEO Characteristics and Firm R&D Spending. Management Science, 48 (1).

Bhagat, S., Bolton, B. J., Subramanian, A. (2010). CEO Education, CEO Turnover, and Firm Performance. SSRN Electronic Journal.

Bass B. M. (1985). Leadership and Performance Beyond Expectations. New York: Free Press.

Bennis, W. G., & Nanus, B. (1985). Leaders: Strategies for Taking Charge. New York: Harper & Row.

Byrne, J. A. (2011). Fortune 100 CEOs: When They Were MBA Students. Available at Poets and Quants: http://poetsandquants.com/2011/05/04/fortune-100-ceos-when-they-were-mba-students/ (consulted May 2017).

Cameron, K., Lavine, M. (2006). Making the Impossible Possible. San Francisco: Berrett-Koehler Publishers.

Gardner, H. (1995). Leading Minds: An Anatomy of Leadership. New York: Basic.

Gottesman, Aron A. and Morey, Matthew R. (2006) Does a Better Education Make For Better Managers? An Empirical Examination of CEO Educational Quality and Firm Performance Available at SSRN: https://ssrn.com/abstract=564443

Khanna, T. Contextual Intelligence. Harvard Business Review, 2014. https://hbr.org/2014/09/contextual-intelligence

Kotter, J. P. (1988). The Leadership Factor. New York: Free Press.
Lindorff, M., Prior Jonson, E. (2013). CEO business education and firm financial performance: a case for humility rather than hubris. Education + Training, Vol. 55 Issue: 4/5.
Mayo, A. J., Nohria, N. (2005). In Their Time: The Greatest Business Leaders Of The Twentieth Century. Boston: Harvard Business School Press.
Podolny, J. M., Khurana, R., Hill-Popper, M. (2005). Revisiting the Meaning of Leadership. Research in Organizational Behavior, Volume 26, 1–36.
The Best Performing CEOs in the World (2016). Harvard Business Review, November 2016.
Velsor E.V., McCauley C.D., Ruderman M.N. (Eds.) (2010) The Center for Creative Leadership Handbook of Leadership Development. 3 Edition. San Francisco: Jossey-Bass.

CHAPTER 4

Class 4: Experience—Three Dilemmas for Would-Be CEOs

Abstract "I learned from classes and from books," says Bob Dudley (CEO of BP, UK). "But most of my knowledge came from my jobs." Every single one of our 20 business leaders—without exception—believes that the trade of CEO must be learned on the job. Formal education provides a useful foundation, they all agree, but the skills you need to secure the top position can only come from experience.

We conclude that the best course of action for future CEO development is to balance breadth of experience with some degree of depth. Ideally, the aspiring CEO needs to start by gaining some expertise before broadening out into new areas. International exposure helps, even though our experts did not consider it as critical as many leadership development experts and academics do. But they agree that it is essential to gain experience of managing people as early as possible, to have had some P&L responsibility before becoming a CEO and to learn by failing! As Jeffrey Immelt (CEO of General Electric, USA) says, "I think business is a game of mistakes... going through cycles, making mistakes and learning from them is what builds character and experience."

Developing profound industry knowledge in the early days of their careers is also very important for effective CEOs. Frontline jobs and positions in operations are essential—ideally in the company you will eventually lead. In the end, according to our interviewees (and all the academic research), the best CEOs usually come from within the organisation. However, an insider must also know how to "stand outside" the company and see it objectively.

© The Author(s) 2018
S. Shekshnia et al., *CEO School*,
https://doi.org/10.1007/978-981-10-7865-1_4

Keywords Failure • Industry knowledge • International exposure • Managing people • P&L responsibility

Güneşte yanmayan gölgenin kıymetini bilmez. (Turkey)
Meaning: Someone who has never been burned in the sun won't know the value of shadow.

Passarinho que voa com morcego dorme de cabeça para baixo. (Brazil)
Meaning: The bird that flies with the bats will sleep upside down. (That is, the experiences you choose will have consequences later.)

There's no arguing with unanimity. And every single one of our 20 business leaders—without exception—believes that the trade of CEO must be learned on the job. Formal education provides a useful foundation, they all agree, but the skills you need to secure the top position can only come from experience.

"I learned from classes and from books," says Bob Dudley of BP (UK), reflecting on his own career. "But most of my knowledge came from my jobs." Or as Constantino Galanis of Química Apollo (Mexico) puts it, from his perspective as a nurturer of other people's talent, "Development should be on-the-job training. Education prepares people. Then you have to put them into the job and let them work, make their mistakes."

But *which* jobs should he put them into? Or, let's put it another way: if you aspire to joining Galanis at the top of the tree one day, which jobs should you seek out en route?

Some companies, of course, have leadership-development programmes. They rotate bright young graduates and MBA holders across departments, divisions, functions and geographies, with a view to fast-tracking them up the corporate hierarchy. But no companies are crazy or brave enough to have specific training programmes for future CEOs. This is one apprenticeship that you have to build yourself. And it's quite a daunting prospect.

Peter Coleman of Woodside (Australia) is typical of our respondents in that he refuses to overcomplicate his role or his trajectory to the top. "The only difference between me and an entry-level person in my organisation is complexity and breadth," he says. "The skills I use today are the skills I started developing when I was 21 years of age. It's like playing junior soccer as a child and then taking that onto the professional field—and finally playing in the World Cup."

Nonetheless, as you start to dribble that ball of skills down the competitive corridors of corporate life on the way to your CEO goal, you will encounter several dilemmas. We'll explore three of them in this class.

4.1   Dilemma 1: Breadth or Depth?

At first sight, this is another question that provokes unanimity. Everyone agrees that CEOs need to develop breadth. Any candidate for the position has to acquire a wealth of experience across different functions (as we glimpsed in Class 3). Sure, you can specialise in finance, operations or IT and still make it to the C-suite. But you'll most likely end up as the CFO, COO or CIO, not the CEO. That job will go to someone who has left the comfort zone of his or her own area of expertise, someone who—ironically perhaps—has proven ability to go back to square one and learn a new skill… several times over.

Those with ambition for the top job need to put together their career portfolios accordingly. An MBA is, of course, a good shortcut to breadth of *understanding*, as we discovered in the last class, but it has to be followed up with breadth of *experience*. Here are just a few of the comments we heard about gaining such experience. And it's rarely a matter of accident:

Shuzo Kaihori (Yokogawa Electric Corporation, Japan): "Variety of careers is a must. The pool of candidates for the position of CEO must have had a variety of careers function-wide or business-wide."

Abdel F. Badwi (Bankers Petroleum, Canada): "It's important not to be just focused in one field and one area, but experienced in several aspects of the business: technical, financial, ability to communicate with people."

Didie Soewondho (PT Wijaya Infrastruktur, Indonesia): "If 'CEO' is understood as a profession like doctor, accountant, engineer, pilot, geologist, etc, then it is too narrow a concept. If it became a profession, a multidisciplinary curriculum would have to be set—with massive case studies of corporate experience."

Renato Bertani (Barra Energia, Brazil): "I came from school with a background in geology, but I had to learn something about engineering, something about statistics, economics, cash-flow modelling, accounting. To be in a leadership role, you have to be multidisciplinary. I think I have been lucky in life, but I made an effort to be multidisciplinary."

In other words, gaining breadth is a matter of design, rather than luck. Maybe it also takes a special kind of person to become a true generalist. As we saw in Class 2, curiosity helps. But humility is also important, as the following fable suggests.

The Fable of the Stupid Questions

Once there was a young woman straight out of business school who joined an oil company. First she worked in marketing. Then she worked in strategy. Then she worked in planning. After that, she became chief information officer (or CIO for short).

"How can you be in charge of IT, when you have no technical background?" some people asked. But they were mainly computing experts who were focused on software or hardware. They couldn't see the bigger picture like the woman (who was not quite so young any more).

Because of her background in strategy and marketing, she knew how different parts of the business *used* the IT systems. And because of her background in planning, she knew how the IT systems *linked up* all parts of the business. What's more, she wasn't afraid to step out of her comfort zone. Above all, she wasn't shy about asking questions.

"Am I so foolish, if I'm asking such basic questions?" she thought to herself. But she concluded she was doing the right thing. After all, she'd never master any new subject without first learning the basics. Instead of giving up on her basic questions, she asked even more—not just to senior people but to quite junior people, putting her faith in them and *showing* them that she was putting her faith in them. This is how she became a good CIO and remained in the job for a very long time.

Eventually, after 36 years in the company, the woman was asked to become CEO. By now, she knew almost everything about the company, so she didn't need to ask so many basic questions. But when she needed to, she didn't hesitate. "How can I make decisions if I don't have all the facts?" she asks.

And that's *not* a stupid question.

Based on our interview with Nishi Vasudeva (Hindustan Petroleum Corporation, India).

Some of our 20 co-authors go so far as to hint that too much expertise in a single discipline can be a drawback. That way lies the temptation to think you know best or, worse, to micromanage someone else's work. No one wants an interfering know-it-all for the boss. "Knowledge of power plants, that's something my engineers manage!" says Yang Wansheng of

China Machinery Engineering Corporation. Or, as Diego Bolzonello of Geox (Italy) explains: "If I have a marketing manager, he must know marketing better than me. If I have a product manager, he must know the product better than me. That's the system. If you feel sick you go to the doctor. If you have legal trouble you go to the lawyer. Specific people must be cleverer than you."

However, that doesn't mean that *everyone* should be cleverer than you. It's important for a CEO not to come across as a dabbler or dilettante: a jack-of-all-trades but master of none. In order to get the most out of listening to experts, you need to understand what it is to *be* an expert. And the experts most certainly won't listen to you, if you have no proven track record in a field of your own.

When we went back to our interview transcripts, we found phrases like "*not only* an engineer" or "*as well as* understanding geology." We concluded that the best course of action is to balance breadth of experience with some degree of depth. Ideally, the aspiring CEO needs to start by gaining specific expertise before broadening out into new areas. Alternatively, he can follow the lead of Nishi Vasudeva (see above) and rotate around a few departments, before focusing for several years on one function.

Jeffrey Immelt of General Electric (USA) has the following advice, which seems to us just perfect:

> Develop careers that are both broad and deep. Broad because it gives you confidence—and deep to every manufacturing technology and customer development. We don't run GE like a holding company, we run GE as an operating company. After my interview today, I'm going to have a detailed product review of one of our businesses and I'll go all the way down from what materials we use to what the customers think. I believe the best careers are deep first, broad second. But over a course of a career, having both is very important.

4.2   Dilemma 2: Home or Away?

In mapping out a path to the corner office, it's clearly important to aim broad, as well as deep. But *how* broad exactly? Is it better to work in many different organisations or even sectors? And what about *abroad*? As business becomes ever more multinational and workforces become ever more multicultural, should you aim to get some experience of working overseas?

Here, the consensus we encountered about developing cross-functional experience starts to break down. In fact, we were surprised by some of the opinions expressed by our CEOs. Given their emphasis on the importance of career breadth, we expected most of them to say that experience across different companies, industries and geographies was preferable to working in the same organisation for a lifetime.

But then, perhaps, we're biased. We've all moved around sectors, companies and countries to some extent. And INSEAD, where we've all worked, is known as the "The Business School for the World." As an institution it places great importance on the value of diversity in the classroom and experience of different perspectives. We believe in the power of diversity in all its forms.

So, it seems, do a few of our CEOs. "I think that a diversified background is definitely essential," says Mazen Khayyat of El-Khayyat Group (Saudi Arabia). "You don't need a CEO who is only dedicated to a certain industry. This will limit the horizon. When he is exposed to other industries—this is what they call 'blue ocean thinking'—he has different inputs. He can adapt them and apply them. Not just interacting with competitors in the same industry definitely gives an advantage."

Similarly, Richard Rushton of Distell (South Africa) insists on the importance of culturally diverse experiences: "The ability to culturally connect with people across the globe—to discover and ask why, to hear new things and see new perspectives. These are incredibly important skills that CEOs need to make sense of the world around them and the companies they lead."

It turns out, however, that Rushton and Khayyat's voices are very much in the minority. But before presenting the majority view, let's take a quick look at Jeff Immelt's route to the top of General Electric, starting from his first post-MBA job.

1982 Enters GE on Commercial Leadership Program
1983 Manager—Business Development/GTX Product Management, GE Plastics
1984 Manager—Dallas District Sales, GE Plastics
1986 General Manager—Western Region Sales, GE Plastics
1987 General Manager—New Business Development and Marketing Development, GE Plastics
1989 Vice President of Consumer Service, GE Appliances
1991 Vice President of Worldwide Marketing and Product Management, GE Appliances
1992 Vice President Commercial Division, GE Plastics Americas

---

(*continued*)

(continued)

1993   Vice President and General Manager, GE Plastics Americas
1997   President and CEO, GE Medical Systems November
2000   President and Chairman-elect, GE. Elected to Board of Directors September
2001   Chairman and CEO, General Electric Company

Immelt's has been a hugely successful career, constructed entirely from experiences in a single company and based largely in a single country (albeit in a global organisation). He joined GE on a generalist training programme and moved rapidly around functions, regions and divisions, spiralling ever upwards to his first general management role, where he lingered a little longer, and from there to his first "CEO" job title as a springboard to leadership of the entire group. It's a pattern we've seen time and time again in our reading, not just of the CVs of our 20 co-authors but of objective, academic research.

In fact, academic research gives a definitive answer. In different countries and in different industries, so-called insiders—CEOs who grew through the ranks within the company—outperform "outsiders"—leaders who landed the top job from the wider market for talent. For example, 84 out of the 100 CEOs in the 2016 *Harvard Business Review* ranking were insiders. And this phenomenon is replicated across large and small businesses, as well as for public and private companies.

Nishi Vasudeva echoes these research findings. "I feel that having a CEO from inside the company is better," she says. "If you are from within the company, you are much more able to relate to the people." After all, companies have cultures, as well as countries do. Those who are from the same culture are less likely to make blunders in their navigation of the organisation. From the recruiter's point of view, there's no guarantee that the internal appointment will be successful, but it definitely improves their chances of not making a costly mistake.

Stefan Messer of Messer Group (Germany) happened to be in the process of selecting a CEO for one of his companies when we spoke to him. "Our CEO of Welding and Cutting is retiring and we have to decide who will be his successor," he told us. "We had two or three outside candidates, but we decided on an inside candidate, because we know his strengths and weaknesses. It helps to have a lot of experience of our business model, our customer structure and the application technologies."

Diego Bolzonello is of the same opinion. "A good CEO in one company could be a really bad CEO in another company," he points out.

Indeed, as we saw in the introduction to this book, the skills needed to turn around a struggling company are very different from the abilities required to keep a market leader ahead of the competition. But it's more than that. Two thriving companies from the same industry and the same country can have such different visions, values and methods that a successful executive in one can be a liability in the other. You only have to look at the many failed examples of mergers and acquisitions across the world to realise this. In 1998, when Jürgen Schrempp, CEO of Daimler-Benz, trumpeted the merger with Chrysler as a match made in heaven, he failed to account for the stark difference in corporate culture between the two apparently similar organisations. The destruction of value over the subsequent decade would turn out to be unprecedented in business history. And the Daimler board got rid of him, before eventually getting rid of Chrysler too.

The impact when the CEO comes from a different industry can be even more catastrophic. John Sculley was PepsiCo's youngest-ever CEO when appointed in 1977 and went from strength to strength until Steve Jobs famously enticed him away with the question: "Do you want to sell sugared water for the rest of your life?" He seemed to be doing well at Apple too, until he ousted Jobs. Yet Sculley's lack of technical insight and instinct caused Apple to lose its way... until eventually he was fired and Jobs returned.

In an ideal world, then, perhaps all CEOs would join a company on a rotational programme for high-potentials. Then they'd move around departments and divisions, acquiring expertise in one function and experience in several other areas—on a steady spiral towards the top. The trouble is, this isn't an ideal world. It's the real world. Many companies don't have developmental programmes for high-potentials. Many do not believe in rotating people across functions. Some are simply too small and vulnerable to allow for any serious leadership development. They're places where people just get their jobs done to keep the company afloat, with no time or space to experiment with new tasks and skills. If that's your case, don't get discouraged. And venture outside sooner rather than later. All the research shows that the earlier an executive makes a move, the higher the chances of successful integration are. Joining an organisation at CEO level carries the highest risk of all.

There are both subjective and objective reasons for that. Most obviously, on the objective side is the knowledge gap that the new CEO and her colleagues at a new company would have to bridge. "To manage a business you need to understand it very well," says Abdel F. Badwi of Bankers Petroleum (Canada). The challenge becomes even more important when it comes to a new industry. "The nature of the industry specifically influences the CEO profile," says Temel Kotil, who was an academic and R&D specialist in a technology company, before becoming the successful CEO of Turkish Airlines. For him, the aviation business is differentiated from other lines of work by its emphasis on emotions and, above all, safety—which is utterly sacred. "You have to get the fundamentals of the industry and you have to spend time with people," is his advice to outsiders.

During the course of our research and teaching over the years, we have come across all kinds of disaster stories about senior executives who failed to follow this simple advice. Miguel Galuccio of YPF (Argentina) tells one such tale of some managers parachuted in after the acquisition of an oil company: "They were bankers," he says disparagingly. "Those people were put there to run a company based on transactions: buy, sell. They had neither connection to the field nor to the oil and gas culture, as we know it. It's very difficult to connect people when you do not speak their language." Needless to say, the acquisition was not a success.

When Galuccio refers to "speaking the language," he is talking in metaphorical terms. But he raises an interesting non-metaphorical point. Should aspiring CEOs invest time in learning foreign languages and gaining overseas experience? "I've seen many people who are excellent CEOs but have no knowledge of foreign languages," answers Vladimir Rashevsky of SUEK (Russia)—who himself has been fluent in English since his twenties.

Of course, there are a few high-profile "foreigners" in charge of large corporations. There are 3 in our sample of 20. But—for all the business world's talk of globalisation—these kinds of leaders still are in the minority. Consider what Yang Wansheng of China Machinery Engineering Corporation has to say: "I have a lot of experience. I worked in machinery for 20 years. That was the period with planned industry, when everything was controlled by government. And during that period of time, I took part in 20–30 projects. I came to this company maybe 13 years ago. And I'm deeply concerned about the development of our country in the future. This is my task, my role." How can an incomer compete with that—either in terms of experience or attitude? It would be like asking Jack Welch (another GE "lifer") to have picked someone other than Jeffrey Immelt as his successor.

Nevertheless, dig a little deeper and neither Yang Wansheng nor Jeffrey Immelt is quite such an insider as at first he seems. Yang Wansheng is a graduate in modern languages, which means he has acquired an external cultural perspective to supplement his long Chinese experience. And Jeffrey Immelt is adamant that his "eyes stand outside the company," as he put it in his conversation with us. "As CEO, you must have the courage to stay outside the company," he insists. "You must have the ability to stand apart. GE has more than 300,000 people. More than two days every year they all hate me!" In other words, a CEO has to be an outsider-insider—simultaneously seeing the company from within and from without.

Curiously also, the only two of our sample of CEOs to have made a successful major transition across industries are—to some extent—insider-outsiders. That is, they found a way to see their new company from an internal perspective. In the case of Temel Kotil, who transitioned from academia to senior business management, there was some luck involved insofar as he had a ready-made network inside the company. "I was a bit lucky," he says, "because, in the ten years before coming here, I taught aerospace engineering. In Turkish Airlines, there were many people who took classes from me!"

In the same way, José Ángel Sánchez of Real Madrid (Spain)—who made the transition across sectors much earlier in his career—deliberately sought out an industry where his previous experience was highly relevant. "I've been working in Real for 12 years now, and before that I worked for Japanese video games company, Sega," he explains. "But it was pretty similar. There you invest in creating content, just as here we invest in the players. Then you sell the content in several different channels—just like we do here. In the end football is a content business too. It was easy for me to adapt."

Ultimately, then, there is some degree of harmony between the authors and our 20 co-authors. We largely agree that would-be CEOs should invest in building a collection of experiences that develops the ability to be both an insider *and* an outsider. Diversity of experience in different companies, industries and cultures can be a *means* to achieving that external perspective, rather than an end in itself. But it's certainly not necessary. If all that seems a little subtle (and our route to this uneasy consensus a little convoluted), here's a simple fable to drive home the point.

The Fable of the Wet Feet

Once there was winemaker from Italy, who travelled across the sea to America to promote his products. While he was there, he decided to go for a walk in the desert. But his sneakers had rubber soles, and it was a very hot day. As he walked, his feet became overheated. The man began to suffer. So he took out his pocketknife and cut holes in the rubber soles, so that his feet could breathe.

The man returned to Italy and forgot all about the holes in his shoes. But the first day it rained he got wet feet. So he bought a new pair of sneakers and set about creating smaller holes—large enough to let water vapour out but too small to let water in. Soon he had created the world's first ever shoes with breathable rubber soles.

Having patented the idea, the winemaker approached many shoemakers to see if they wanted to buy his invention. But none of them understood it. They wanted to keep on making shoes the way they always had. "Why should they listen to winemaker?" they said.

And so the winemaker became a shoemaker. First he made shoes for children only. Then he started making shoes for men and women. His company grew and grew and grew until it had more than 4,200 employees, 1,600 shops and €875 million in annual revenues. Nearly 25 years after the walk in the desert and the wet feet, it is one of the biggest shoe companies in the world.

The moral of this fable? A winemaker *can* become a shoemaker. In fact, he may even become better at his trade than a shoemaker who only sees his business from the inside.

Based on our interview with Mario Moretti Polegato, founder of Geox (Italy)

4.3   DILEMMA 3: NUMBERS, PROJECTS OR PEOPLE?

"My professional life took me to certain positions very young," reflects José Ángel Sánchez. And so it is for most successful CEOs—including the others in our sample of 20. Along with multidisciplinary experience and an inside-out perspective (see above), early responsibility is essential. But what are the most important management rungs on the CEO ladder? Leadership development specialists insist on early P&L responsibility, experience of managing teams and undertaking change initiatives as the most important building blocks of future business leaders. Many scholars highlight the critical role of life's crucible in leadership development. Let's see what our experts have to say on this subject.

Chul-Kyoon Lee of Daelim Industrial Co. (Korea) observes: "Career management is very important and it depends on what your company is doing. In order to manage an engineering company, you do need engineering knowledge, but you also need human resources knowledge. And the third most important thing is financing. These are the three minimum qualifications for a CEO."

Bob Dudley has essentially the same list but puts the three elements in a different order, starting with finance (and related skills), then knowledge of the company's inner workings and following up with people management:

> There are some universal knowledge blocks: legal responsibilities and constraints, investor relations, finance, industry knowledge. If you do not know these you cannot be a CEO. You also need to know how to bring it together, how the corporate machinery works. It is very important and very hard to figure out. Even very talented people who have not worked in HQ have difficulties to understand it when they become CEO. And of course you need to motivate people, to align them, to lead them. This does not come from a course.

Vladimir Rashevsky seems to have the exact same set of priorities for experience—stated in the same sequence as Dudley—even if the words he uses are slightly different:

> When it comes to basic competences, executives need, first of all, financial management: the ability to control the company's finances. It is also important to be familiar with the markets where the company operates and to have a detailed understanding of the technologies and production processes the company deals with. As for skills, it is important to have a certain level of emotional intelligence.

Meanwhile José Ángel Sánchez appears to place more emphasis on the human than the financial. "In the end it's the bottom line of the company, so you need to understand technically how things work in financial world," he says. "But, apart from that, everything is more on the human side, in my opinion."

Who are we kidding? There's no point in trying to manufacture a debate here. It's a matter of common-sense consensus, surely. You need *both* financial and human experience and expertise to become a CEO. Or, as summarised by Diego Bolzonello, "People with no leadership experience cannot be a CEO. They must practise to understand what it means to be a leader. But a CEO without any capacity to understand the numbers... very difficult! You can't make any decision without the numbers." In short, there's no point in attempting to prioritise one over the other.

Nevertheless, there is clearly some tension between managing stakeholders and balance sheets. It's a theme that runs subtly throughout all of our interviews. And it's the reason why the bankers in Miguel Galuccio's sad tale of a failed acquisition (which we saw above) ultimately came unstuck:

> They were distributing dividends for 85% of the net income they had in Argentina, because they had loans and they could not send cash out of the country. I understand that can be the right thing to do, because you have an international portfolio. You want to take the cash you produce in Argentina and put it in other places to make a better business. But they forgot about managing one of the main stakeholders, that is, the country where they worked—where 80% of the company's cash was produced.

Realistically, in most industries and corporations, any ambitious, young "high-potential" is going to get people management experience well before P&L responsibility. Management of a division or country will likely be the last piece of the career jigsaw to slot into place before the final promotion. But, as Galuccio warns, the earlier lessons learned mustn't be forgotten. Or, as he so nicely puts it, by way of moral to his tale, "As CEOs, we have to remember we are in the shop where we are working for others. Those others are stakeholders and we need to be able to identify all of them and make sure we create value—probably a different kind of value for everybody we work for."

Here perhaps, as so often in business, the 80–20 rule applies. Jean Sentenac (Axens, France) is the only person to quantify the question of people versus numbers: "A successful CEO spends 20% of his or her time on strategy and finance, but most of it with people: employees, clients, shareholders." Again, the message is that the numbers and people are both important but that the former shouldn't eclipse the latter. Here's one final fable to inspire you.

The Fable of the Family and the Firm

Once there was an engineering student, who set up a small workshop making acetylene lamps. Over the years, he expanded his business to include other devices and other gases. For more than half a century, through two world wars and a global depression, he continued to grow his company. Just before he died, he handed it over to his son.

The son expanded the company yet again. It became part of an economic miracle that advanced the entire nation. He formed alliances with other companies—some of them abroad—to make the business even bigger. But then the growth stopped. So the founder's son decided to merge with another company.

Now the family owned only a third of the firm, but they remained in charge and all went well. After a big wall in the country was knocked down, new markets were opened up, and the company thrived once again.

By now, it was time for the founder's son to retire. He found a CEO from outside the family to take over, and the growth accelerated—on a global scale. The new CEO was mostly interested in money and abandoned the old family values of caring for customers and employees that had guided the company. He took many risks to try and make more money, which eventually resulted in ruin. He was forced to step down, and the company was sold very cheaply to a bank.

The new financial investors were *only* interested in money. They used words like "restructuring" and "debt relief." They were very surprised when one of the founder's grandsons offered to buy their shares, because the company still wasn't making much money. "Why would he want it?" they thought. But they sold it to him anyway.

Of course, the financial wellbeing of the company was one of the new CEO's main concerns. But he spoke a very different language from the bank. His new mission statement was: "We act sustainably to meet the needs of our customers in accordance with our collective responsibility for people, progress and the environment." And guess what? The family, the company and the stakeholders prospered—and lived happily thereafter.

Based on our interview with Stefan Messer (Messer Group, Germany) and the history of the company documented on messergroup.com.

4.4   In Conclusion: How to Learn from Experience

This class has been all about collecting experience on the way to the top. The previous class was all about collecting education on the way to the top. But learning from experience isn't at all the same thing as learning from education. Education is about getting things right, while experience is also about getting things wrong. And—as we glimpsed in Class 2—there's much more to be learned from failures than successes. Here's what Jeffrey Immelt has to say:

> I think business is a game of mistakes. Business is not about perfection. I think that going through cycles, making mistakes and learning from them is what builds character and experience. Business is all about trying things, learning, trying again, learning from experience, getting better. We fire people if they make the same mistake twice, but I think you have to tolerate a certain bandwidth of experience building. And it's particularly important for CEO to have been through these cycles and know what works—and what doesn't work.

For the next generation of CEOs, the experience of failure will be more important than ever before, because of the sheer pace of technological change. Shuzo Kaihori (Yokogawa Electric Corporation, Japan) is eloquent on this point:

> Don't follow past successes, because our industry, IT, is changing every day. Other industries are changing too, if more gradually. People see past success and try to do the same things. We must always see with fresh eyes.

The dilemmas set out in this class are nothing compared to the dilemmas you will face if you finally become a CEO. You will not always get the answer right. Just make sure that you learn from failure, so that you keep your eyes eternally fresh.

Some Further Reading

Bennis, W. G. (2009). On Becoming a Leader. 4th Edition. Philadelphia: Basic Books.

Conger, J. A., Benjamin, B. (1999). Building Leaders: How Successful Companies Develop the Next Generation. San Francisco: Jossey-Bass.

Conger, J. A. (2010). Leadership Development Interventions. Ensuring Return on Investment. In: R. Khurana, N. Nohria (Eds.) Handbook of Leadership Theory and Practice. Boston: Harvard Business School Press.

Drucker, P. (1999). Managing Oneself. Boston: Harvard Business School Publishing.

Kets de Vries, Manfred F. R. (2017). Riding the Leadership Rollercoaster. Palgrave Macmillan.

CHAPTER 5

Class 5: Meta-Skills—a C, E and O Taxonomy

Abstract Those who aspire to reach the C-suite must use their experience to develop certain mental capabilities and patterns of behaviour. The main insight to take away from this class is that anyone can develop effective leadership practices well before they reach a senior leadership position. In fact, you do not even need to be a manager to hone the three essential CEO habits outlined in this chapter.

In CEO School, we group the key skills into C-thinking, E-acumen and O-learning. And our 20 co-authors insist on the importance of developing all three as early as possible. C-thinking involves an ability to see the wood from the trees and to master complex, critical, creative and constructive thinking. E(motional) acumen is first about recognising yourself as human (that is, with emotions and needs, such as the desire for respect and fairness) and regulating your behaviour to satisfy your emotions. Second, it's about recognising that others are human too—and using the resulting insights to build and maintain the social relations that create value for the company: in short, empathy. O-learning combines openness to learning with its operationalisation and an ongoing determination to continue learning throughout life.

Keywords C-Thinking • Development • E-acumen • Meta-skills • O-learning

Jack of all trades, master of none. (USA)

Qui n'avance pas, recule. (France)
  Meaning: Someone who does not move forward, goes backwards.

Breadth, depth and variety of experience—as covered in our last session together—are essential for anyone serious about making it to the top job. Sadly, though, they're not enough to make you CEO ready. You must also *use* your experience to hone your skills. The main insight to take away from today's class is that anyone can acquire senior leadership skills well before they reach a senior leadership *position*. In fact, you don't even need to be a manager to practise the essential abilities outlined in the next few pages. For ease of understanding and remembering, we've grouped these competences together into three meta-skills: *C-thinking* (complex, critical, creative and constructive cognition), *E-acumen* (emotional expertise) and *O-learning* (operationalising new insights). As this class is arguably the most important of our entire course, we've divided it into three sessions that you can complete at your own pace.

Before we dissect our three umbrella skills into their component parts, however, we'd like to make a short historic detour. As we mentioned right at the beginning of this book, the academic study of leadership began with so-called great man theories. The central assumption was that effective leadership was a product of special people who were different from normal mortals and possessed unique, innate characteristics. This approach lost its appeal, when experts began to realise that there were many apparently great men—in possession of all the leadership traits they'd carefully identified—who were nonetheless incompetent at running companies. As time went by and business education developed, so the researchers' emphasis shifted from "traits" to specific managerial skills. Hence the first of our higher-level competencies and the first of our three sessions.

5.1   Session 1: C-Thinking

5.1.1   *What Is It?*

Sometimes in our classes and coaching sessions, depending on the focus, we refer to this as "business acumen" or "systemic thinking." But it's basically about understanding how the various cogs in an organisation work together to function as an entire machine—and also how they mesh with cogs in other external machines. At its most fundamental level, you could say C-thinking is all about seeing the wood for the trees—or the bigger picture. But it's more than that. It's about seeing how the trees combine to make up the wood: the interconnections between the people, departments, infrastructure and other component parts of a company. And it's about understanding the whole forest ecosystem too: the industry, the value chain, the national context and the global economy. And about generating ideas that will bring about change without destroying the system. Richard Rushton of Distell (South Africa) sums this up neatly.

From Seeing the Wood to "Smelling the Field"
The longer you serve as a CEO, the greater the danger that you do not see the wood for the trees. Leading a company is about holistic thinking: how various parts wake up the whole system and the rules of impact on the system, as well as the ability to make realistic · changes in the system. It's an incredibly important and complete skill that I believe all CEOs require. The ability to manage conflicting requirements and requests for resources is based on the ability to use holistic thinking. In the end, this also gives you the ability to understand facts quickly, based on smell of the field. Great CEOs actually use intuition in arriving at their decisions about prioritising and allocating organisational efforts and resources.

What's interesting about Rushton's insight is that he focuses on both the intuitive and the analytical aspects of a CEO's C-thinking. Or, as the great psychologist (and Nobel Laureate) Daniel Kahneman has dubbed it: "thinking fast" *and* "thinking slow." Similarly, Constantino Galanis of Química Apollo (Mexico) believes that the mark of a great CEO is his ability to "take all the information… and use his gut feeling to make the necessary decisions."

But others, such as Diego Bolzonello of Geox (Italy), home in on a more analytical and methodical approach. "A company is a system," he says. "And a CEO approaching the system is like a doctor examining a human body." We encountered this analogy so many times during our interviews that it is clearly significant. And the person who dwelled longest on it was Temel Kotil of Turkish Airlines (Turkey). This is what he said.

The Anatomy of an Airline
Turkish Airlines is a system—like the body is a system. There are different organs that work together, and they have certain purposes. And the most crucial thing for a healthy company is the relationship between them. As CEO and as management, our duty is to clean up, like a doctor, before the sores become cancers. Now, there are 18,000 people in Turkish Airlines—and they have daily problems. There are conflicts and conflicts of interest, even though we have very solid ethical rules. I cannot follow what everyone is doing like the police! And many of them might be cleverer than me (we have 60 PhDs in this company). But my duty is to clean up, make sure that everything is working smoothly. A successful CEO is one who puts things in order, challenges the strategies *and* the young minds— and puts it all together. In addition, it's important to keep the body working hard, otherwise it becomes unfit.

Doctors, of course, don't make snap, intuitive judgements—unless they're faced with an emergency (there'll be more about crisis management in the next class). Whenever time allows, they think slow instead of fast. They analyse a patient's symptoms, past medical history and environmental factors in all its complexity. They then construct a theory out of the known data, using a certain amount of creativity to fill in any gaps. Next, as true scientists, they criticise their own conclusions, testing them against reality. In our classes and coaching sessions with business leaders we focus on four elements of C-thinking.

- **Complex thinking** is about demonstrating "helicopter vision"; understanding interconnections between various aspects of business and organisations; identifying critical success factors and risks in strategy, business plans and projects; effectively evaluating both short-term and long-term effects of management decisions; seeing the influence of commercial activities on the whole business. "The larger and more complex a company is, the wider and more profound the CEO's skills should be," adds Vladimir Rashevsky of SUEK (Russia).

- **Critical thinking** is about questioning assumptions and solutions; coming up with independent ideas; withstanding intellectual pressure. Very importantly, critical thinkers challenge their own assumptions and brainwaves. "You have to be your own worse critic," as Jeff Immelt of General Electric (USA) puts it.
- **Creative thinking** is about demonstrating curiosity, striving for new ideas, experimenting, accepting failure and learning from it, borrowing ideas and solutions with ease. "The first goal for me is to be creative," confirms Yang Wansheng of China Machinery Engineering Corporation (China).
- **Constructive thinking** is about striving to answer "how?" rather than "why?", transforming ideas into business plans with established controls and metrics, demonstrating knowledge of commercial trends in both local and global markets, considering them while planning campaigns and strategy, effectively overcoming shortage of resources. "You need to know how to *bring it all together*," explains Bob Dudley of BP (UK).

Outstanding CEOs are masters of all four components of C-thinking, as summed up in the following diagram (Fig. 5.1).

5.1.2   *Why Does It Matter?*

It's pretty obvious why C-thinking matters for CEOs. They're in charge of a complex business after all. And they have to deploy all their critical, creative and constructive faculties to juggle the various complexities in such a

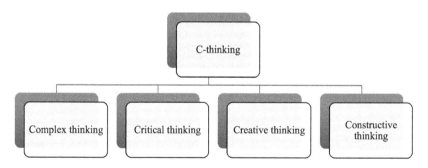

Fig. 5.1 Four components of C-thinking

way as to sustain (and hopefully improve) the company. Miguel Galuccio of YPF (Argentina) expresses this situation in terms of keeping all stakeholders happy.

> **Balancing Your Stakeholders**
> It is important that you never feel so successful that you isolate yourself. As a CEO you are working for different stakeholders and understanding of who the stakeholders are is very important. Your stakeholders are also your investors. And in my case it is more difficult, because I have private and public investors—and I have to work with all of them at the same time. Then the communities where you work are also your stakeholders. And of course, your people are key, but that includes the unions too. As a CEO, you have to execute and give results, but you cannot forget about the environment and your different stakeholders. Being able to manage that balance is the key recipe for success.

However, Galuccio's list of examples omits some key stakeholders, such as suppliers and their employees—and perhaps the most important character in any business story: the *customer.*

"We once had a CEO who never visited customers," reflects Stefan Messer of Messer Group (Germany). "Why to visit customers? There's no need to visit customers... I have my people for doing that, yes?" And he laughs, before recalling that the CEO in question didn't last long. In other words, if you want to keep your job as a CEO, C-thinking is not only useful but essential.

What's more, it's never too early to start developing C-thinking. Of course, as a junior employee, you will have quite narrowly focused targets and key performance indicators, but the better you understand the reasons these goals were set in the first place, the more likely you are to achieve them. At least, this is what our 20 conversations with CEOs indicate.

5.1.3   Have You Got What It Takes?

We can't tell you whether you're already an expert at C-thinking. But we can help you to reflect on the way you think. Here's a quick exercise to get you started. Take ten seconds to look at this famous painting. Then turn over the page and write down a few sentences about what you saw (Fig. 5.2).

Fig. 5.2 *The Hunt in the Forest* by Paolo Uccello (c. 1470, Ashmolean Museum, Oxford)

Now let's interpret your description.

Is it about details of the picture? Did you write about medieval hunters, dogs, horses and trees? If so, then we can assume that you are a detail-oriented thinker. Most CEOs are good at this too. But they're also big-picture thinkers (or have learned to be), which is absolutely essential for their job. The good news is that you can train yourself to thinking more systemically, by working out how the parts contribute to the whole.

Or is your description about the picture as a whole? Maybe you mentioned a forest and/or hunting scene with effects of perspective, colours, style and your general impression? In this case you may be a big-picture thinker. You see the whole as well as the parts... like most CEOs. But you could probably learn to think even more systemically, by figuring out the intimate connections between the parts and the whole.

(For those who are curious about the even bigger picture, the artwork is *The Hunt in the Forest* painted by Italian, Paolo Uccello, around 1470. It's one of the earliest examples of the use of perspective in painting, and you can see the original in the Ashmolean Museum, Oxford.)

5.1.4   How Can You Do Better?

In theory, people who grew up in Asia should perform better than anyone else on the above test. It's often said that Eastern thought patterns are holistic, whereas Western mindsets are atomistic or reductionist. The origins of these traditions go back some 2,500 years, when the ancient Chinese philosopher Confucius laid down his rules about family and collective harmony. Meanwhile in Europe, the ancient Greek atomists were trying to reduce the world to its smallest constituent parts, setting the scene for modern science—which is still discovering ever-smaller sub-atomic particles and has drilled down from genetics to epigenetics.

Confucianism still influences cultures such as Japan, Korea and Vietnam, as well as China, Singapore and Taiwan. So we weren't surprised to hear some of our Asian CEOs taking a more holistic approach to their roles than their Western counterparts. In many ways their attitude sets an example to us all.

"We have to think more about some kind of macrocosmic view and some kind of bigger problems, and that's why we pay big attention to the problems of the whole world," says Yang Wansheng of China Machinery Corporation. "The global economic crisis or falling GDP in China... these can influence our projects and competition in the whole world. This kind of knowledge is something that I have to continue grasping."

Across the Sea of Japan, Shuzo Kaihori goes one step further. For him it's not just about how the external environment affects his business, but how his business affects the world beyond it in a vast interconnected web of impacts. He observes: "I have a strong belief in the value of Japanese culture. We are taught that in business three parties have to be happy— seller, buyer, society. If your customer is successful, then society is success- ful and the CEO is successful too. We are not *trained* in this, but it is the Japanese culture for running a business. It helps me to make decisions and to be a better CEO."

Thus from our Asian CEOs, we can learn to look beyond the narrow confines of our organisation to the entire industry, the whole of society, the environment, the legal context and the global economy. Even if you're many years away from becoming a CEO, you can put yourself in the shoes of your competitors and ask yourself what market strategies you'd adopt. And when travelling for business or pleasure, you can actively develop a more holistic view of the world. Take time to learn about different cul- tures, learn new languages and try to answer key questions. How is this culture different from my own? How might this affect the way people behave in a corporate setting?

If you don't have the good fortune (or budget) to travel the world, make a point of consuming an international diet of media, whether websites or television channels such as BBC World, CNN, Al Jazeera (from the Middle East), France 24 and others. The goal is not to change your views but to shift your perspectives: to see your own culture from outside and where it fits in the world.

On the other hand, holistic thinking has its limitations. As we saw ear- lier, C-thinking involves analysing the whole into its constituent parts— and putting them back together again. And here, if cultural theorists are to be believed, Western CEOs like Bob Dudley might have a natural edge. "There are some universal knowledge blocks: legal responsibilities and constraints, investors' relations, finance, industry knowledge... If you do not know these you cannot be a CEO," he says, adding: "You also need to know how the corporate machinery works. Even very talented people who did not work in the HQs have difficulties to understand it when they become CEO. You need to live through a corporate cycle to figure it out."

While you're living through that corporate cycle, there are many other strategies that you can deploy to improve your C-thinking. The most obvious of these is to map your stakeholders and make time for them. Meet with both customers and suppliers regularly and ask probing ques- tions. It's particularly enlightening to find out how they compare your business with those of your competitors. If you're already very senior, you can do the same with venture capitalists and financial analysts, that is, the people who influence the share price of your business.

Above all, to cut a long and complex story short, no matter how junior you are, you need to start investigating how exactly your job contributes to your company's success, as well as how it dovetails with other jobs in other departments. And this habit needn't stop at the reception desk of your organisation. Truly systemic thinking extends to all stakeholders, especially customers. Of course, you will have your own narrowly focused targets and key performance indicators, but you'll perform better as an individual if you seek to understand the collective reasons those goals were set in the first place.

All this advice is highly analytical, of course. But the more methodically you practise this kind of thinking on the way to the top, the more intuitive it will be when you actually get there. Not that we're suggesting you ditch the analysis, once you're in charge. Business leaders need to question their intuitions, as well as their assumptions. It's just that time will be your most precious resource of all as a CEO. So anything you can do to speed up your own decision-making will reap rewards.

5.2   SESSION 2: E-ACUMEN

5.2.1   What Is It?

At this point in the class, let's return briefly to our detour through the academic history of leadership. To sum up the story so far in one sentence, the "great man" theory of leadership eventually gave way to a "competency-based" model centered largely around technical skills. However, after a few decades, academics began to realise that many poor leaders were taking the trouble to gain all of the technical skills that business schools and books could supply… and remained poor leaders. Leadership was clearly much more intricate than simply acquiring and deploying a specific set of so-called business competencies.

Sometime in the 1980s, the academics started focusing once again on the question of "who leaders are." They started to combine the old ideas about personal characteristics (though not necessarily the traits once attributed to "great men") with the newer ideas about technical skills. Finally, in 1995, Daniel Goleman published his best-selling book *Emotional Intelligence*. Here he argued for the importance of understanding and regulating personal emotions, reading the emotions of other people and taking into account the emotional condition of others in social or business interactions. In fact he went so far as to quantify so-called EQ claiming that the abilities that make up emotional intelligence count for twice as much as technical skills and general IQ put together, when it comes to business leadership.

Needless to say, leadership experts and psychologists have been arguing about emotional intelligence ever since. But there's no doubt that Goleman's book has had a strong and positive impact on humanising executives, who now learn their assistants' kids' names, say "thank you" to subordinates and even participate in 360-degree feedback exercises. Today, nearly all respectable organisations have their own model of leadership competencies, which include some elements of emotional intelligence alongside technical skills.

Personally, we don't question the usefulness of Goleman's model, but we prefer to think in terms of "E-acumen" (or maybe E-Qumen?) rather than "emotional intelligence" (EQ)—in order to emphasise that emotional and empathetic expertise can be acquired—and we've simplified it slightly as follows. Basically, E-acumen is first about recognising yourself as human (that is, with emotions and needs, such as the desire for respect and fairness) and regulating your behaviour to satisfy your emotions. Second, especially for a CEO, it's about recognising that others are human too—and using the resulting insights to build and maintain the social relations that create value for the company: in short, empathy (Fig. 5.3).

Fig. 5.3   E-acumen

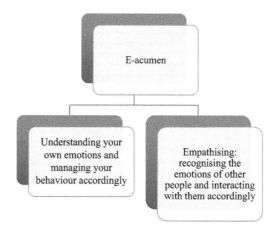

5.2.2   Why Does It Matter?

So far, so straightforward. There's no doubt that the academic concept of emotional intelligence has had immense practical value in the real world. And there's no dispute among our 20 CEOs either. In fact, none of them question the importance of emotional acumen for their work. Here's Temel Kotil again.

Think with Your Heart

In the airline business, *especially* in the airline business, you need a big heart, besides professional skills. Emotions are more important, because they pay you back in the same day, with good things and bad things. And sometimes I behave emotionally. I just support what passengers and employees need—this is simple mathematics.

This morning, for example, I arrived from my hometown. I saw that the airplane was very crowded with a lot of fuss going on at the back. I asked the head flight attendant what was happening, and she said that a family of six or seven had come late and couldn't be seated all together. The aircraft was full of workers, but there was plenty of space in business class. So I asked her, "Why don't you upgrade some people?"

She upgraded the family members, who were very happy of course. And we lost nothing, because we always have additional food always in business class. Really, if you want to gain success in the airline business, your employees should take the side of the passenger. This is what I mean by having a big heart.

Like Kotil, José Ángel Sánchez of Real Madrid (Spain) claims that emotional E-acumen is particularly important in his own industry. "Everything is pure emotion in a football club or the computer games industry, so you need a certain emotional intelligence to be the leader," he says.

But emotion seems to matter in even the most seemingly unemotional sectors too. "The skill of being able to lead technically, emotionally, ethically for me is the key," says Miguel Galuccio from the oil industry. "Human skills are very important," says Jean Sentenac from the world of technology. "The human side of being a CEO is the most important aspect," says Constantino Galanis (chemicals). "I think you need a lot of human skills, social skills to lead a company," says Stefan Messer (industrial gases). "For any CEO," concludes Vladimir Rashevsky (energy again), "it's important to have a certain level of emotional intelligence."

Amidst all this agreement, however, we did find one interesting and salient point. When our conversations drilled down further into the concept of E-acumen, we found a near-universal emphasis on one particular aspect of it: communication. Indeed, for Mazen Khayyat of El-Khayyat Group (Saudi Arabia), leadership and communication are synonymous. "I believe that leading people is a matter of communication," he says. "The ability to manage, motivate and work with people, interact with them is summarised in the ability to communicate."

However, communication is also one of the most misunderstood skills in the entire history of leadership. Most people assume it's all about issuing crystal-clear instructions, explaining strategy and providing diplomatic feedback, in such a way that people feel motivated and empowered. And of course a CEO does need to have this ability. "I know very few successful CEOs who don't have a powerful ability to communicate clearly to their organisations," says Richard Rushton.

However, speaking and writing (that is, communicating *to*) are only half of the story. No one will never develop emotional acumen if they don't first learn to listen—and truly *hear* what others are saying. The story about the family upgraded to business class (as recounted by Temel Kotil above) underlines the importance of this distinction. The flight attendant asked the passengers what they were making a fuss about, but she didn't act until the CEO had made her take note of the complaint, internalise it and find a solution.

It goes without saying that CEOs must listen to *all* stakeholders, not just customers—and most of all the senior management team. Mazen Khayyat once again explains it perfectly.

Listen with Your Heart
The CEO should never take a risk beyond the appetite of the stakeholders. He should never stop listening to his team. He should never stop trusting the team, because that gets back to the team—which means they stop trusting him and no longer feel obliged to perform and deliver. He should never stop being human, because it's human to care—and compassion is necessary to working with people. It's the *art* of working with people.

Listening also has its practical benefits. "It would be very bad if a CEO thinks he knows everything," says Jean Sentenac. "He has to be open and to be able to listen to people. This is what I mean by human skills."

Of course, not all forms of human expression are spoken aloud. Listening also takes place with the eyes or intuition, as Constantino Galanis explains: "A CEO must be alert, with eyes wide open all the time." And he continues: "He must have a very good team around him that will consult him and tell him what they feel." Or, as Diego Bolzonello puts it, "the biggest mistake is to decide against other people."

To sum up, then, emotional intelligence is essential for today's CEOs. And by far the most important component of it—based on our conversations with practising business leaders—is *empathy*.

5.2.3   Have You Got What It Takes?

We don't know you, so we can't assess your emotional acumen. But we can help you to start thinking about your own abilities. You'll find below some statements designed to reflect different aspects of your life and work. Choose the number from the scale −3 to +3 that best reflects your attitude to the statement and write it down.

−3	−2	−1	1	2	3
Fully disagree	Mostly disagree	Partly disagree	Partly agree	Mostly agree	Fully agree

1. I'm well aware of my strengths and weaknesses.
2. I usually keep my cool under pressure or when criticised by other people.
3. I like listening to other people talking about their lives.
4. If someone compliments me on my appearance, I try to return the compliment.
5. I notice the first signs of my irritation before someone else points them out to me.
6. I have my own personal ways of getting myself out of a negative mood.
7. Colleagues would describe me as a good listener.
8. Friends would describe me as the life and soul of the party.
9. I can easily describe to others what I feel at any given moment.
10. Others consider me a person who can effectively manage my emotions.
11. Even if I'm really busy, I'll make time for a friend who needs a shoulder to cry on.
12. I know how to cheer up other people.
13. When I make a choice, I listen to my gut feeling
14. Difficult conversations don't easily upset my routine.
15. I can usually judge people's moods from their facial expressions or the atmosphere in the room.
16. I am able to resolve emotional conflicts between people.

Now transfer your points to the table below, add up your total for each line and then calculate your overall score.

Self-awareness	1 ____	+	5 ____	+	9 ____	+	13 ____	=	_____
Self-regulation and control	2 ____	+	6 ____	+	10 ____	+	14 ____	=	_____
Empathy/understanding other people's emotions	3 ____	+	7 ____	+	11 ____	+	15 ____	=	_____
Social skills/managing relationships	4 ____	+	8 ____	+	12 ____	+	16 ____	=	_____
						Overall score		=	_____

Now for your results! It goes without saying that you should not treat them as definitive. After all, completing the exercise accurately requires a certain amount of emotional acumen in itself. Instead, consider both the exercise and the results as a way to start thinking about your skills in this area.

Score for each component

- 9 and above: this is one of your strengths—congratulations, but don't be too complacent about it!
- 2 and below: this is an area to concentrate on in your personal development.
- Scores in between: you are like most human beings in this respect—which means there's definitely room for improvement.

Total score

- 40 and above: you are a master of emotional acumen—but don't take this for granted!
- 9 and below: you clearly underestimate the power and influence of emotions, and there's plenty of work to be done.
- Scores in between: unsurprisingly, you are like most human beings in terms of your emotional acumen—which means there's definitely room for improvement.

5.2.4   How Can You Do Better?

Clearly, empathy and other aspects of emotional acumen come more naturally to some people than others. But the good news is that all of us, whoever we are, can become more emotionally astute by learning to listen.

The earlier you start the better. And listening is not only a skill to develop as you rise towards the giddy heights of the CEO's office—as a means to acquiring the empathy you'll need when you get there; it's also a faculty to continue honing at the top.

One simple method of improving your listening skills is to attend a meeting where you would normally be contributing and to volunteer instead to take on the role of an observer or process consultant. Force yourself to just listen. Afterwards, as well as passing on valuable observations and conclusions to your colleagues, you can ask them how the normal dynamic of the meeting changed as a result of your silence.

"Active listening" is a term given to a number of techniques that enable you to truly hear what people are saying. It involves paying full attention, using your eyes to read body language as well your ears to hear what's being said—"between the lines" as well as overtly. You can also use your own body language to show the speaker that you're paying attention, making eye contact and appropriate gestures like nodding and smiling, yet being careful all the while not to interrupt the flow, distract the speaker or become distracted. Once you've finished listening, remember what's been said and reflect it back at the person you're engaging with, by using their words for your own contribution or paraphrasing their meaning to demonstrate that you've understood. Defer judgement until you're satisfied that your interlocutor has finished and disagree only if you have to—with respectful honesty.

Ultimately it's fine to disagree, but if you jump in with interruptions and pre-prepared counter-arguments, you're not really listening. And if you're not listening, how can you possibly be empathetic? The great benefit of active listening is that—if you get it right—you're modelling a kind of behaviour that will encourage people to listen more carefully to you. And the more they listen, the more you can reveal of yourself, building trust through transparency. If there's one thing better than empathy, it's mutual empathy!

As well as practising active listening until it becomes instinctive, aspiring CEOs should also seek regular feedback on the impact of their behaviour on others. Performance reviews are useful, certainly, but they generally take place only once or twice a year. Asking other people, whether your superiors, direct reports or peers, for their assessment of your performance should be a weekly or daily habit, even if the answer may not always be easy to hear. In addition, you should reflect on this feedback to determine how you could improve in your weaker areas. Eventually, you will find that you begin picking up signals without having to ask questions, while adjusting your behaviour becomes instinctive.

Another useful strategy is to pick one of your customers to be a focus of your personal attention for a period of, say, six months. Make it a point to visit this customer regularly so that you get to know his or her concerns intimately and establish a strong relationship. This is a practice that we particularly recommend for senior managers and new CEOs, who often get so caught up in internal politics and what the competition is doing that they lose touch with the person who matters most in business: the customer.

5.3   Session 3: O-Learning

5.3.1   What Is It? And Why Does It Matter?

The listening techniques described above are only of use if you are constantly *open* to learning—both about yourself and the business (and beyond). And of course, learning for its own sake is all very well, but it's of no practical benefit unless you *operationalise* the most valuable lessons. Even this is of limited help to you as a CEO unless you also apply your best discoveries in an *ongoing* fashion. Hence the term O-learning—or *optimal* learning, if you prefer.

In fact, no matter how complete your business thinking and how strong your emotional acumen are, these two skill sets count for nothing unless you are prepared to acquire more of them. The trick—especially for those who are very senior—is to use every experience as a source of learning, sucking up knowledge and trialling new competences in everyday situations. Cast your mind back to Class 2, where we discovered the importance of curiosity and exploration, and to Class 3, where we discovered the value of university-level study as training for further learning. Remember too, Class 4, where we discovered the importance of using experience to gain industry knowledge. Now, it's time to put all of these into practice, as described by Vladimir Rashevsky.

The Broad Horizons of Self-Improvement
There is always an opportunity to study. Ideally managers should know how to study those areas in which they do not work but which are important. They may be somewhere on the horizon or may not relate to the business of a given company. But you have to be inquisitive and try to study other subjects in depth. Having access to a wide range of knowledge allows you to test new approaches, which may have never been tried in your area before. All sources, whether journals, books and analytics, are useful for your general understanding of a subject. But after that, you should address a primary information source, someone who provided the data for those journals, books and so on, meet with them, ask questions and then try to stay current with what's happening in this area. This is the basis of a CEO's self-improvement in both the personal and professional domains.

Rashevsky is clearly talking about learning *as* a CEO, not learning to *become* a CEO. But the habit of such high-level learning is best developed while you still have plenty of spare time and you haven't developed other—less comprehensive—learning habits. So, what do CEOs learn and how they do it? As we saw earlier in this class, Bob Dudley defines the "universal knowledge blocks" of the CEO as legal responsibilities and constraints, investor relations, finance and industry knowledge. But here's how we choose to break down the key elements of CEO learning, followed by a more detailed explanation of each area of expertise (Fig. 5.4).

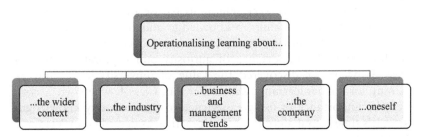

Fig. 5.4 Operational learning

The Wider Context CEOs make big decisions that have a long-lasting impact on their companies and their companies' stakeholders. To do this effectively they need to understand the environment in which the company operates today—and will operate tomorrow. One caveat here: in different companies "tomorrow" means different things. For an organic juice bar, it's probably next season, while for a large energy company, it's more likely to mean five to seven years from now. And in any case, there are also many challenges with the environment today. The first is that it's so big! Even if you run a small hotel in the South of France, your business is affected by digital technology, oil price dynamics, terrorist attacks in European capitals, stock markets in major global cities, Donald Trump's policy initiatives and much more.

The second challenge is that the context is forever changing—and the pace of change is only increasing with time. This means that you have to keep learning about the business environment on a continuous basis not from time to time. Chul-Kyoon Lee of Daelim (South Korea) concludes: "As CEO, I need to forecast the future to have a corporate foundation for both shareholders and employees." Alas, however, only you can decide where best to concentrate your efforts. But your own industry is a good place to start....

The Industry Although the borders between industries blur as "blue oceans" open up and create new markets, the notion of sectors still remains relevant for most companies. The CEO should get to know the customers, competitors, suppliers, technology and regulators that define the sector—and constantly update his or her own mental models of what constitutes the industry. This knowledge cannot come from only one source and requires great personal engagement. The worst mistake is to leave the intelligence gathering to subordinates or a marketing department. Although these are important sources of information, the CEO should have his or her own access to primary sources. The CEO should meet with customers, speak with competitors, visit suppliers and attend technology conferences.

Knowing what's happening in adjacent industries is also a must for today's CEO, since they are a potential source of both interesting ideas (about products and technological solutions) and bad news (in the form of new competitors). And in some sectors, this external perspective is particularly important. "In our industry," says Shuzo Kaihori of electronics company, Yokogawa (Japan), "the CEO also has to understand the trends in technology *and* its influence on society." Above all, however, the leader of the organisation must understand the trends in business and management thinking....

Business and Management Trends In today's world, business is a knowledge-intensive undertaking. There are millions of companies constantly looking for better ways to service their customers, allocate their resources, optimise their assets and enhance the productivity of their people. Every CEO should try to keep up with the latest thinking—whether at the airport bookshop or in the business school classroom—and try to apply it to his or her own organisation....

The Company In our combined decades of experience, we have never met a CEO who knows his company well enough! Assets, technology, working methods, culture and, most importantly, people should be objects of the leader's constant attention and interest, without of course descending into micromanagement. Good CEOs combine "big-picture" understanding with a "detail-oriented" approach to their organisation, with a particular focus on key people at different levels of the company—their motivations, dreams, skills, strengths and shortcomings. And there's one person who's particularly key....

Oneself As we discovered when we progressed from C-thinking to E-acumen, knowing oneself is vital. We'll leave the last word on what and how to learn to Jeffrey Immelt.

> **Leadership Is a Journey into Yourself**
> One of the first things I always say to people in GE is that I think leadership is an intense journey into yourself. It's how fast you want to learn, how strong you can be. You have to be demanding on yourself, you have to be a self-starter, you have to look in the mirror every day and you have to be extremely critical—and yet at the same time know yourself and be self-confident again.

5.3.2   Have You Got What It Takes?

By virtue of the fact that you're reading a book about how to become a CEO, we assume that you're pretty open to learning! But here's another exercise to help you assess this skillset in a more detail. This time, decide how well you match each statement and add up the resulting scores.

1. I love to read reports and analytics that are relevant to the industry and markets I work in.

Very much like me	5
Like me	4
Neutral	3
Unlike me	2
Very much unlike me	1

2. I prefer to rely on my personal managerial experience.

Very much like me	1
Like me	2
Neutral	3
Unlike me	4
Very much unlike me	5

3. When I get a new project, I can't wait to start working on it.

Very much like me	5
Like me	4
Neutral	3
Unlike me	2
Very much unlike me	1

4. I think my work could be more exciting.

Very much like me	1
Like me	2
Neutral	3
Unlike me	4
Very much unlike me	5

5. The idea that we now ought to study all our life sounds attractive to me.

Very much like me	5
Like me	4
Neutral	3
Unlike me	2
Very much unlike me	1

6. **Much of my professional knowledge has become obsolete.**

Very much like me	1
Like me	2
Neutral	3
Unlike me	4
Very much unlike me	5

7. **I would consider taking online courses or training in a subject that interests me.**

Very much like me	5
Like me	4
Neutral	3
Unlike me	2
Very much unlike me	1

8. **I don't go out of my way myself to attend conferences or forums—especially if they're overseas.**

Very much like me	1
Like me	2
Neutral	3
Unlike me	4
Very much unlike me	5

9. **The world seems to me a breathtaking place.**

Very much like me	5
Like me	4
Neutral	3
Unlike me	2
Very much unlike me	1

10. **I quickly get bored with routine.**

Very much like me	1
Like me	2
Neutral	3
Unlike me	4
Very much unlike me	5

My total score is _____.

If you scored from 40 to 50, you probably love learning and tend to teach yourself if no one is around to help you. Most CEOs are like that too. But, as you're a self-starter when it comes to learning, we're sure you want to know how to do even better....

If you scored from 20 to 39, you like to learn and understand the importance of renewing your knowledge and skills.

If you scored from 10 to 19, you're probably not a natural autodidact, but you could become one. And you'll need to if you're going to be a successful CEO!

5.3.3   How Can You Do Better?

Immelt's observation about a "journey into yourself" applies as much to learning as it does to leadership. Research shows that the key to effective adult learning (which every CEO should master) is the practice of self-reflection. Many decades ago, the original management guru, Peter Drucker, identified a number of techniques that effective leaders use on a regular basis. One of them was reflection.

The reason self-reflection is so important for CEOs is that there's only so much you can learn before you're in post. "I was around John Browne for quite some time, when he was in charge," says Bob Dudley, referring to a previous, well-respected leader of BP. "I saw everything, but I could not understand the board-CEO dynamics, the importance of succession and compensation issues or how to deal with them."

According to Drucker, all good leaders regularly find time and a quiet space to sit down and reflect, asking themselves questions about their past plans and assumptions, actual events and lessons to be learned from them. Typical CEO questions are thus: What did I plan? And what actually happened? How do I explain what happened? What should I change in my mental models and in my actions on the basis of this experience?

The sooner you start setting aside moments to ask such questions, the faster you will master the art of reflection. Working with coaches and mentors will also help to hone this skill as well as to learn from it. Usually it is not that difficult to find a mentor, someone who can provide regular formal or informal advice. To start with, this will probably be a senior colleague from the same organisation or a similar professional background. But more experienced managers are likely to look further afield.

"I think there is a strong role for outside perspectives and mentoring from other industries," says Richard Rushton. "This helps a CEO to see the world slightly differently."

Seeing situations from the outside is a particular benefit of coaching, which is a form of professional development that several of our CEOs recommend—especially for those who are already in management roles. "There are now a lot of what is called coaches," explains Abdel F. Badwi of Bankers Petroleum (Canada). "They are people who have communication skills—somebody you meet once a month. You discuss some issues, test how you have handled some situations, talk about some outcomes that did not turn out the way you wanted... and find out why. If you want to continue enhancing your leadership skills, engage a coach."

Peter Coleman of Woodside (Australia) is one of the greatest advocates of professional coaches that we encountered on our travels. Here he describes his personal experiences of both coaches and consultants as sounding boards for learning.

Coaching as a Long-Term Commitment

What leading sportsperson or team would dream of trying to win a gold medal or the premiership without a coach? So why, in business, do we think we can be consistently successful without a coach? I've used personal coaches several times in my career. I have a personal coach now—and the same coach works with all my executives. It's someone I've worked with on and off for 30 years. I think you have to surround yourself with people who know you and whom you respect, people who know how to communicate with you. You have to feel comfortable enough in the relationship for them to challenge your assertions and paradigms.

Now, does that coach help us with strategy? Usually not, because that's more what consultants are for. I also widely use consultants to understand my business, whether for recruitment or strategy. I've developed relationships with people who know both me and my business, to ensure that they understand the things that I'm trying to achieve and understand my values, as well as bring an independent view.

As well as coaching and mentoring or simply learning from consultants and colleagues, there are all kinds of options for continuing professional development—whether through industry bodies, corporate universities, training providers or business schools. "As a company identifies people that have leadership qualities, they can continue their education by providing seminars and courses to learn about leadership," says Abdel F. Badwi.

As in the case of experience (see Class 4), the trick is not to become "siloed" in your options, to achieve breadth of learning as well as depth. By all means, choose a specialist programme, but check to see whether there are sessions on leadership, as well as technical skills.

We would also add, based on our own long association with business schools, that prospective CEOs need to be proactive in seeking out formal learning opportunities. Whereas once HR departments singled out "high-potentials" and suggested leadership programmes in the way that Abdel F. Badwi describes, we find that more and more participants on short courses at INSEAD have taken the initiative and *asked* for support (or just unpaid leave) to attend. Even an off-the-shelf leadership programme becomes *self*-directed learning if you seek it out for yourself.

However, even if you have no mentor, no coach, no opportunities to attend executive education and no in-house training programme, you can still study on your own. The CEOs we encountered during our research seemed to know instinctively how to turn every experience and every source of information into a form of learning. Exploration is an everyday habit for them: they push back intellectual boundaries and hoover up knowledge everywhere they go, before enhancing it with self-reflection and applying the results to their business.

Be warned, however. There are two types of self-reflection. You can either challenge what you already know or seek to confirm it. A good CEO always does the former.

5.4   A FINAL WORD

By way of conclusion to the three sessions of Class 5, here's a final cautionary anecdote from Stefan Messer about the ill-fated CEO (mentioned above): the one who didn't last long because he failed to take an interest in customers. It seems he wasn't much interested in his staff either....

"When he started," says Messer, "I made a trip with him to Latin America, because we had a lot of activities there. We visited our affiliate company in São Paulo for a business meeting and then had three hours before our plane left. We went to the meeting room, where we were sitting and reading the newspapers. I told him, 'Why don't you go with me to the offices? We'll say hello to people, we'll look at what they do, we'll ask them about their work—and whether they're happy.' I convinced him to come with me. We made our rounds and everybody was very pleased. He didn't know how to do this and yet he was the big boss. But he learned it there."

Unfortunately, if you wait until you are "the big boss" to learn these lessons, it may be too late—as turned out to be the case for Messer's CEO. In this single incident, he managed to demonstrate a lack of complex business thinking (how does the affiliate company work and thus contribute to the parent business?), a lack of emotional acumen (how are people feeling about their work?) and a lack of openness to learning (you can't gather firsthand industry intelligence from a newspaper). Without C-thinking, E-acumen or O-learning, no wonder he didn't last long as a CEO.

Some Further Reading

Bower, J. (2007) Solve the Succession Crisis by Growing Inside-Outside Leaders. Harvard Business Review.

Chatman, J. A., Kennedy, J. A (2010) Psychological Perspectives on Leadership. In: R. Khurana, N. Nohria (Eds.) Handbook of Leadership Theory and Practice. Boston: Harvard Business School Press.

Drake, R. M. (1944) A study of leadership. Character & Personality. 12, 285–289

Finkelstein, S. & Hambrick, D. C. (1996) Strategic Leadership: Top Executives and Their Effects on Organizations. West Publishing Company.

Goleman, D. (1995) Emotional Intelligence: Why It Can Matter More Than IQ, Bantam Books.

Goleman, D. (2006) Social Intelligence: The New Science of Social Relationships, Bantam Books.

Groysberg, B., Kelly, K. L. & MacDonald, B. (2011) The New Path To the C-Suite. Harvard Business Review.

Hitt, M. A. & Tyler, B. B. (1991) Strategic decision models: Integrating different perspectives. Strategic Management Journal, Vol.12 (5).

Hollenbeck, G., McCall, M. W., and Silzer, R. F. (2006). 'Leadership Competency Models'. Leadership Quarterly 17 (2006): 398–413

Kaplan, S. T, Klebanov, M. M. & Sorensen, M. (2012) Which CEO Characteristics and Abilities Matter? The Journal of Finance. Volume 67, Issue 3.

Kets de Vries, M. & Engelau, E. (2010) A Clinical approach to the dynamics of leadership and executive transformation. Edited by N. Nohria and K. Khurana. Harvard Business School Publishing.

Kets de Vries, M. (2002) Can CEOs Change? Yes, But Only If They Want To. INSEAD Working Paper Series.

Rotemberg, J. & Saloner, G. (1998) Visionaries, Managers, and Strategic Direction. Harvard Business School.

Senge, P. (1990) The Fifth Discipline: The Art and Practice of the Learning Organization.

Smits, J. S. & Ally, N. Z. (2003) "Thinking The Unthinkable" — Leadership's Role In Creating Behavioral Readiness For Crisis Management. Competitiveness Review: An International Business Journal, Vol. 13 (1).

Tappin, S., Cave, A. (2010) The New Secrets of CEOs: 200 Global Chief Executives on Leading.

Wooten, L. P & James E. H. (2008) Linking Crisis Management and Leadership Competencies: The Role of Human Resource Development. Advances in Developing Human Resources, Vol. 10 (3).

CHAPTER 6

Class 6: Roles—The Four Essential Functions of the CEO

Abstract "I was around John Browne for quite some time, when he was in charge," says Bob Dudley (UK, BP). "I saw everything, but I could not understand the board-CEO dynamics, the importance of succession and compensation issues or how to deal with them."

There's only so much that aspiring CEOs can rehearse before taking the job. Their development will continue once they're in the spotlight on the centre stage. And they'll grow into their CEO-specific roles much more quickly if they understand exactly what's required before they start work.

The trouble is, there's a vast industry dedicated to making business leadership seem highly complex. Business schools, strategic consultancies, headhunting firms, training providers, coaching practices... they're all built on it. Fortunately, however, our 20 CEOs see their role in much simpler terms. And it reduces to four essential—but interrelated—tasks: envisioning, nominating, enabling and managing crisis.

Keywords Enabling • Envisioning • Crisis management • Leadership coaching • Nominating

Нет плохих судов, нет плохих ветров, есть плохие капитаны. *(Russia)*
Meaning: There are no bad ships or bad winds, only bad captains.

توصــــه ولا حكيمــا أرســل *(Saudi Arabia)*
Meaning: Send a wise man and don't advise him. (That is, if you pick the right person for the job, they should know what to do.)

© The Author(s) 2018
S. Shekshnia et al., *CEO School*,
https://doi.org/10.1007/978-981-10-7865-1_6

If this book were your career, you would be just starting out on your first CEO posting. Congratulations! You have nurtured the skills of Class 5 to the point that they're instinctive—and you're ready to apply them on a whole new stage.

Don't overdo the celebrations, however. Although there's only so much you can rehearse before the opening night, you will grow into the part much more quickly if you take time to understand exactly what's entailed *before* you step into the spotlight.

The trouble is, there's a vast industry out there dedicated to making business leadership seem more complex than it actually is. Business schools, strategic consultancies, headhunting firms, training providers, coaching practices... they all have a tendency to mystify the work of the CEO. Fortunately, however, our 20 practitioners see their jobs in much simpler terms. And it reduces to four essential roles: *envisioning, nominating, enabling* and *managing crises.*

In this class we'll describe each of the roles in detail, but more importantly we'll share some specific practices our co-authors and other effective CEOs use to enact them on the business stage. You may adopt some suggestions and reject others, but by the end you will have a full range of practices to choose from. Think of this chapter not so much as a class but as four "coaching sessions," one for each role, which don't all have to be consumed in a single sitting. In keeping with your more senior status, we'll be using traditional coaching instruments of framing, questioning, rephrasing and recounting stories, rather than telling you what to do. We'll also use comments from our 20 CEOs to provide coaching-style "feedback."

How Leadership Coaching Works

As business leadership becomes more and more complex, new and prospective CEOs are increasingly turning to coaches to help them grow into their roles. Business coaches create a safe environment for you to see yourself more clearly and try out new ideas and behaviour. They *frame* the topic, ask focused *questions* and tell *stories* that stimulate ideas. This is what we'll be doing in this chapter. Good business coaches *challenge, rephrase* and *reflect* back your answers and observations. They provide individualised *feedback.* Above all,

(*continued*)

(continued)

they *listen*. We can't do that from where we're sitting. You'll just have to imagine one of us being there, helping you to *clarify your goals*, *define new ways of behaving* and *commit to results*. It's not such a ridiculous idea, because a coach can only ever be a catalyst and a sounding board. It's the person being coached who really has to do the work. All the same, we'd recommend not relying on imaginary coaching! It's much more effective to find a real experienced professional through a professional body, personal recommendations or the coaching network of a business school.

6.1   COACHING SESSION 1: ENVISIONING

Our 20 CEO experts needed no prompting to talk about "vision." It's a topic nearly all of them raised spontaneously. "The ability to define an accurate vision is *very* important," says Jean Sentenac of Axens (France). "You need to give a clear vision of where you want to go, where the company wants to go—and some business objectives," explains Renato Bertani of Barra Energia (Brazil). And for Abdel F. Badwi of Bankers Petroleum (Canada), the "role of the CEO is *mainly* about vision."

This enthusiasm for vision is not surprising given its prominence in the literature on leadership—both academic and practitioner-focused. More interesting and insightful are the subtleties in the descriptions of the CEO's work in defining, articulating, communicating and updating company vision, that is, in playing the *envisioning role*.

Contrary to the widespread theoretical view of a corporate vision as a picture of the future set in stone, our CEOs consider vision a work in progress. Fine-tuning and updating the corporate vision is a never-ending process of unravelling a paradox. This is how we—as your unofficial coaches—would frame it.

- First, good vision is *crystal clear* at any given moment, yet it is also *evolving* along with the company and the macro and micro environment in which it operates. As Diego Bolzonello of Geox (Italy) says, "Direction is made by a long-term vision…and you modify it continuously, because in this environment you need to understand what is happening all around the world. That's really the main role of the CEO."

- Second, good vision is *objective*, reflecting the realities of the context, the business, its assets and its people, yet it is also *subjective*, reflecting the changing mental models, ambitions and goals of the CEO. "Don't get excessively pulled or pressurised by external impulses," warns Nishi Vasudeva of Hindustan Petroleum (India). "Be very clear to yourself about where the company needs to go and how it needs to get there."
- Third, good vision is grounded in *rational* evaluation of the market and business potentials, yet it must also be *inspirational and emotional*. Renato Bertani explains: "It's not about sending orders out; it's really about making people believe you know the right way and providing the right vision."
- Fourth, good vision provides *direction* and establishes fundamental working principles for *everyone* in the organisation, yet it leaves plenty of room for *creative* expression from every *individual*. As Lee Chul-Kyoon of Daelim (South Korea) says, "Once a system is set up, it will function. But if we don't all *share* the same future perspective, it won't work. The CEO provides that."

As you can probably see by now, developing (and updating) the company's vision is a challenging task, which requires huge intellectual and emotional effort, time and creativity from the CEO. Fortunately, as your leadership coaches, we can recommend a number of specific practices to help with it—all based on questioning.

Constructing your own theory of where your business environment is headed is a good start. Diego Bolzonello explains it this way: "A real CEO must have a vision of what will happen in the market, the space you want to occupy. And how to get there." Here are some basic questions to help.

Coaching Questions to Help You Predict the Future Context of Your Business
- What will happen to the world in the next five or ten years?
- What major trends will emerge? And how they will impact my business?
- Are we in a growing or declining industry?

(continued)

(continued)

- Where will the growth come from?
- What will happen to existing competitors?
- How vulnerable are we to non-industry competition?
- How will customers' tastes and products evolve?
- What will happen to technology? And what impact will it have?
- How will the available talent pool look in ten years?
- How will the government's role change?

The questions above should provide you with just a few ideas. As Jean Sentenac puts it, "You have to anticipate, feel that something is going to change and move the entire company in that direction before any of your competitors get there. That kind of anticipation is very important." It goes without saying that answering these basic questions won't be easy, but the abilities you enhanced in Class 5 (to learn, to collaborate and to think systemically about both your business and your industry) will make it enjoyable! And you don't have to be the CEO to start coming up with answers.

The next important step is to articulate your ambition to yourself. Ideally, you should begin this process long before the three magic letters C, E and O adorn your business card. But it's never too late to start thinking about where you're headed.

Coaching Questions to Help You Clarify Your Personal Ambition
- What is it that you really want to achieve? And by when?
- What are the three most important characteristics of the company of your dreams?
- How would this organisation look from different points of view: financial, operational, reputational and cultural?
- What are you ready to sacrifice time with family and friends for?
- How do you want to be remembered?

Giving honest answers to questions like these will help you to put your ambition into concrete words and possibly numbers. But a corporate vision will encompass much more than personal ambition. It will also be driven by your own and your organisation's values.

Formulating your personal and professional principles is another exercise you can try long before you become a CEO. This shouldn't be a problem if you've mastered the self-reflection we discussed in Class 5. You can also ask people who know you well: your spouse, parents, children, friends and former colleagues. But, if you are already the boss, don't ask your current colleagues. Most likely they will say what they think you want to hear! If you need any prompting, simply type "values list" into Google— and you'll come up with hundreds of examples to choose from. Here are some more coaching questions to make the selection process easier.

Coaching Questions to Help You Define Your Personal and Professional Values
- What guiding principles do you never compromise on?
- When you are faced with a tricky situation, what moral or professional guidelines do you use to find a solution or to make a decision?
- How would you like others to describe your principles?
- Which of your own qualities do you most appreciate?

After you have made your list, compare it with the values of your company. They may be written in gold letters above the reception desk downstairs or not articulated at all, but every organisation has some core norms that regulate the behaviour of its members and some shared basic beliefs that keep it together. How far apart are the two lists? Do you have enough stamina to bring them together? Where should you push your values, and where is it OK to settle for the corporate status quo? As Richard Rushton of Distell (South Africa) claims, "It's as much about shaping the culture that will realise the vision as the vision itself." In some ways, corporate vision and culture are inseparable.

Assuming you really are a CEO, you're now ready to articulate your vision. Armed with your "picture of the future," articulated ambition and values, you can start writing. But before you put pen to paper, let's get one thing clear. We're not talking here about an official corporate "vision statement" of the kind that most big companies display on their websites or the inside covers of their annual reports. These tend to be heavily word-smithed and excessively pithy expressions of the company's ambitions—

usually produced with the expensive intervention help of a branding agency or similar. But, as coaches, we're more concerned with what's going on in the CEO's brain—and how he or she turns such thoughts into words—followed by strategy and action.

Apple is a rare example of a company that doesn't have an official vision statement, although the following words by CEO Tim Cook are often quoted instead:

> We believe that we are on the face of the earth to make great products and that's not changing. We are constantly focusing on innovating. We believe in the simple not the complex. We believe that we need to own and control the primary technologies behind the products that we make, and participate only in markets where we can make a significant contribution. We believe in saying no to thousands of projects, so that we can really focus on the few that are truly important and meaningful to us. We believe in deep collaboration and cross-pollination of our groups, which allow us to innovate in a way that others cannot. And frankly, we don't settle for anything less than excellence in every group in the company, and we have the self- honesty to admit when we're wrong and the courage to change. And I think regardless of who is in what job those values are so embedded in this company that Apple will do extremely well.

Rather than reproducing a whole series of such statements from well-known CEOs or yet another set of questions, we'll provide a story about one of our coaching clients.

Five Years to Be the Best
Our client—let's call him Alex—was working as a management consultant, when he was invited by the founders of a privately owned conglomerate in an emerging economy to join them in a senior executive role. After a series of acquisitions, they decided to create a stand-alone energy company, and Alex was the natural choice for CEO, even though he was only just about to turn 30. He'd gained everyone's respect, thanks to the professionalism and commitment to learning and development (which he openly espoused as some of his personal values).

(continued)

(continued)

The young CEO's brief was simple: turn this collection of assets into a business... without any extra capital. But Alex was more ambitious than that. His vision was to create the best-run company in the country in terms of performance, systems, management, talent and reputation.... within five years. He wanted the business to be an employer of choice, supplier of choice and (given his brief from the owners) *borrower* of choice. He shared all this with the organisation.

On a more personal level, his ambition was to prove himself as a CEO and make his family proud of him. But it was more than that. The company's HQ was in the region he came from, not the nation's capital. He wanted to build his hometown's economy and prove that it could be home to a great company and attract executives of a top international calibre.

In his first year, attracting top executives is exactly what he set about doing. At the same time, he put in place a transparent system of reporting, as well as improving the performance of the company's various components by reducing waste and cutting costs. All the while, however, he was also seeking to understand more about the context of the new organisation—not just now but in the future. To some extent this was made easier by the fact that the owners had set some clear guidelines and the regulators provided many more. He reasoned that the industry was likely to remain highly regulated for the foreseeable future and that foreign competition was unlikely to pose a threat, partly because of the nature of the business and partly because growth prospects in the region were modest.

In his second year, Alex concentrated on building the newly recruited talent into a team—and consulting them on all key decisions, as well as reaching out to people in all parts of the organisation. He also invested in new technology and introduced modern policies, procedures and governance practices. By now, he'd also realised some of his own limitations, notably in image and public speaking. So he got himself a coach, some new suits and attended courses at INSEAD and Harvard.

(*continued*)

(continued)

By the third year all the basics were in place. Alex was able to refine his vision and focus on more sophisticated practices, such as company-wide talent development and health, safety and environmental (HSE) management. There were further performance improvements too, this time thanks to sales, marketing and public relations innovations—including the creation of a company magazine and frequent coverage in the national media. Alex himself was often interviewed, but—for all his newfound public speaking skills—he was careful not to do all the talking. He went around the company to hear what employees had to say—and around the world to benchmark with other energy companies.

By the fourth year, the company had adopted some world-class practices. There was a corporate university, a bottom-up innovation programme and a new compensation system for managers, based on both performance and development. Alex was not only investing in the training of his people but of his suppliers and customers. Based on his recommendations, the board also reorganised the corporate governance system.

By the beginning of the fifth year, Alex had received several awards for being the country's best CEO, and the company had been ranked the national top employer for two years in a row. The management team had also won an award for being number one in the country. And the shareholders were making a 30% annual return on their investment. The vision had become a reality a whole year ahead of schedule. Now it was time for the young CEO to define a new one…

As you can see, Alex was very clear about assessing the future business environment, as well as defining his personal ambition and values. He also chose to set a five-year vision and used it to attract talent and define strategic goals.

Just how far ahead your own vision should stretch is a matter of opinion and also depends on the company, sector and geography. "A minimum of five years. Without a horizon of five years you cannot develop the company," says Diego Bolzonello. But Jeffrey Immelt of General Electric (USA) ups the stakes. "It's possible to make a projection of what the world is going to be like in 5, 10, 15, 20 years," he says. And Lee Chul-Kyoon goes even further: he claims to be looking 120 years ahead!

When you have articulated a vision you are happy with, try it on other people from different levels of your organisation: direct reports, middle managers, rank and file employees and key external stakeholders such as shareholders. Unlike Alex, many inexperienced CEOs often forget the last of these, but our experts insist on their importance. "You're not going to be successful in raising capital for your company unless you have a strategic vision," as Renato Bertani points out.

See if different parties get it, if it resonates with them and if it motivates them for action. If it does, you have a real thing. If not, keep working on it. Naturally, there may be some rolling of eyes and scepticism about "another corporate strategy and PR exercise." But don't be put off, unless people really start disagreeing with the ideas you're expressing. And don't be afraid to argue your case, either. Alex's experience wasn't always easy, as many people thought that his five-year schedule seemed overambitious. But in the end, his own determination and belief won the argument. As Peter Coleman of Woodside (Australia) puts it, "You have to engender a sense of purpose within the organisation that is enduring and self-motivating to the point where the CEO doesn't have to be there!"

Communicating your vision to the organisation is arguably the most essential part of the *envisioning* role. We would like to offer you four proven CEO practices for doing so, each of which is also demonstrated in Alex's story:

- One of our clients calls the first practice a "walking vision," which comes from the idea of "walking the talk." But we just call it *personification of vision*. In other words, the CEO becomes a living representation of what her vision is about. If it's about excellence, the CEO strives to excel in everything she does. If it's about collaboration, she makes collaboration her way of work. If it's about technology, the CEO becomes the company's chief technology advocate. Diego Bolzonello sums it up: "You must be an example to others and understand the meaning to them of your actions." In any case, as Nishi Vasudeva says, you'll soon be found out if the "integrity of your words and actions" isn't clear, at which point you'll lose the trust from colleagues that you need to be effective. In Alex's case, he demonstrated his commitment to becoming the best by going back to school himself.

- The second practice is sometimes called a "talking parrot." But it simply boils down to *reiteration of vision*. Good CEOs use every opportunity to articulate their vision: regular management team meetings, corporate conferences, shop-floor walkabouts and occasional encounters in the office corridors. They may use different words each time, but keep sending the same message about where the company is going and what it stands for. This is exactly what Alex did in his consultations with his management team, his workforce, the owners and the board. Then he used every issue of the company magazine and his media interviews to repeat his vision once again.
- The third practice is *operationalisation of vision*. According to Richard Rushton, the CEO is "fundamentally required to *shape* the future," and part of this future is internal. Corporate rules, policies and procedures, working methods and products... they all speak without having a mouth—and effective CEOs make good use of them to promote the vision. Meanwhile, the least effective business leaders ignore them and often end up with conflicting messages— one that goes from the CEO's mouth and another that the existing compensation policy delivers. If your vision is "to be number one in the world in the shoe business," as Diego Bolzonello claims for Geox, you have to make sure that you reward excellence rather than mediocrity. And you must recruit and promote ambitious people, giving them freedom to create and innovate. Alex, for one, operationalised his vision through the new compensation package and the creation of a corporate university designed to develop and retain talent.
- The fourth practice is *instrumentalisation of vision*. Nishi Vasudeva describes it as follows: "a broader vision and a feeling for external factors, so that you can fix difficulties, as they arise." To explain this more fully, good CEOs encourage their people to use the corporate vision as a benchmark for all kinds of decision-making. When your VP of marketing asks for advice about who to hire as head of marketing for Northern Europe—an INSEAD MBA with two years' experience working for your main competitor or an industry veteran—your first question back to him should be: "Who would fit our vision better?" The same logic applies to investment projects, acquisitions or divestitures, and new products or services. Which choice will bring us closer to our vision? Which one would reinforce our values? These are the questions managers in your company have to ask

before making any decisions. If they do, your vision has become instrumental. That is, it is working as a management tool. Under Alex's management, for example, his vision became the key criterion for selection throughout the organisation.

In addition, of course, a well-formulated vision allows the CEO himself to make effective decisions. As we'll see in our third coaching session (on enabling), good CEOs these days make as few decisions as possible, but there are situations when *only* the CEO can step in and make a choice for the organisation. In the words of Jean Sentenac, "Vision is also about having courage in difficult situations. Most operational decisions are already taken in organisations—and often decisions that come up relate to conflicting situations—which means that the job of a CEO is a job of doubts. When you take essential decisions, you are not always sure you are right. You may not see the results for several years, but you have to make a decision now."

We'll leave the last word to Peter Coleman, who uses a metaphor for the role of the CEO that we encountered several times on our travels (perhaps even more often than the image of the CEO as a "doctor" or "anatomist" that we saw in Class 5):

> The CEO is the captain of the ship: the person who is standing up on the deck, looking at the weather on the horizon and charting the course. To do that, CEOs need to understand the company's capabilities and the competitive environment—and they need to make good strategic choices. That's an imperative. They need to have strong inner conviction and strength, because it's a lonely spot. And they need to make decisions to ensure consistency of purpose.

The Idea to Take Away from Coaching Session 1

Setting, communicating and updating a vision for the business is the first and foremost role of the CEO. This vision provides the rest of the organisation with direction, meaning and culture—and becomes a benchmark for decision-making for all managers. It may evolve but needs to be deeply embedded in the entire organisation at all times.

6.2   COACHING SESSION 2: NOMINATING

Another client of ours is responsible for a remarkable corporate turn-around. What was once an "airline to avoid" became a dynamic premium carrier within five years of him becoming CEO. As soon as he was appointed, he let go many senior executives and replaced them with younger, less experienced managers. It took 18 months for his management team to stabilise and start performing. The operational and financial results followed, but he kept changing one of the functional VPs, even though each incumbent seemed to be doing well enough. When asked why, he answered without hesitation: "I have to be a hundred percent confident in every person on my team. What if a crisis strikes?" He finally found the right person… just before the crisis struck. By the way, this VP was a great help during the crisis and eventually moved on to become CEO of a subsidiary.

What do we learn from this story? To start with, the CEO is indeed the captain of the corporate ship, as Peter Coleman suggested at the end of our previous session. The leader is largely responsible for choosing the destination and setting the course of the company. But that also means selecting an outstanding crew to keep the vessel on the right bearing. This is the second key role identified by our school of CEOs. We'll refer to it as "nominating," but it's also known as "scouting for talent" or just "selecting the right people."

In playing this role, the CEO matches key jobs with people, identifies talent within and outside the organisation, and helps high-potentials to develop and mature. As we'll see in the next session (on enabling), nominating comes into its own in modern organisational models, where the leader no longer makes all the decisions and controls their execution but helps others to do so. Human talent has become the major asset of most companies, and the CEO must be the ultimate master of it.

The nomination role is crucial for sustainable business performance. If a CEO recognises and plays this role well, her organisation will end up with motivated, competent and autonomous professionals in key positions. The paradigm of "distributed leadership" creates superior human capital that—when working at full capacity—delivers superior performance.

We'll conduct this coaching session a little differently from the previous one. Having framed the idea of nomination, we'll now present you with "ten commandments" for effective nominating derived from conversations with our co-authors and our own professional experience. We'd like you to review them and then answer a number of questions.

The Ten Commandments of Nomination
1. **Thou shalt invest time in the task and never stop looking for talent.** Allocate at least 20% of your time to evaluating talent and making people decisions—and this doesn't include time for developing or mentoring your staff. Keep your eyes open at work, at home, at a football game and on the beach. Then remember what you saw and return to scoop up the best people when the time is right.
2. **Know thy people and what makes them fit the company.** Be clear what you're looking for. Define it in a few simple terms: traits, values or characteristics. Three to five specific requirements are enough, but avoid generic factors such as communication skills, general intelligence or business acumen. Concentrate on what's unique to your company instead. And if a person doesn't quite match your description, but you strongly feel she's right for the job, give your instincts a chance (while also testing them for the possibility of unconscious bias). Make her an offer.
3. **Thou shalt occasionally hire from the outside purely for talent (not necessarily for a specific job).** Don't worry about matching external hires with a specific job, if they fit with your company and have potential for growth. When you see real talent, go for it.
4. **Know thy core positions**—and fill them. In most companies the jobs which make a critical contribution to the creation of value are not limited to CEO −1 and CEO −2 levels, they may be deep in the organisation. Knowing and personally staffing them is an imperative for any CEO.
5. **Give functional jobs to people who are stronger than thee in that discipline.** Diego Bolzonello sums this up best: "When we select people, they have a function and I have a specific rule. They must be better than me in that function!"
6. **Give jobs to people who have the potential to succeed thee one day.** You know from Class 4 that the best way of developing leadership skills is to allow people to lead, so don't waste any precious opportunities.

(*continued*)

(continued)

7. **Always make development a part of thy nomination decision.** When you promote people define their developmental programme in the same way as you define their responsibilities, authority and accountability. "When we choose someone to be a top manager, we proceed with the process of training. It's obligatory," says Yang Wansheng of China Machinery Engineering Company (China).

8. **Move thy people into new jobs for potential not for readiness.** Nobody is ever 100% ready for any job. Take risks by promoting people with potential. Stretching assignments are good for leadership development.

9. **Keep thy people for performance not for potential.** Motivation and potential open the doors to key jobs, but it's performance that keeps people in the room. Make this clear to your managers and act swiftly if they don't start to perform after the entry stage is over (admittedly, the length of this period will be different for different companies, industries and positions).

10. **Do not be afraid to nominate thy tricky or troublesome people.** They may not be easy to work with, they may have challenged you in the past, they may not dress to your liking, but they will bring diversity, originality and dynamism to your team.

And, for good measure, here's an 11th commandment especially for CEOs who are moving on....

11. **If thou must move to another company, thou shalt not do it alone.** Research shows that changing companies when you are CEO is a very risky business. Bringing your team along is a moderating factor. But what will happen to your former company in this case? Better to stay where you are and reinvent yourself, perhaps.

Now, after you have studied our commandments, take some time to think about them and your own experiences of selecting and appointing people. Here are some questions that may help you:

- Which commandments resonated with your experience and views?
- Which commandments went against your experience and views?
- Which commandments came as a surprise?
- Which commandments do you actually use?
- What prevents you from using the others? Is it about the commandments (not relevant, not effective, simply wrong) or yourself (not aware, no time, no resources, no skills)?
- Which commandments would you carve into your own tablets of stone? Which would you leave out?
- Are there any other commandments that you'd add to your own list?
- Can you think of two or three things you could start doing or stop doing to improve your effectiveness in playing the nomination role (even if you're not yet a manager)?

We hope you had something to say about each of the questions, especially the last three. We don't believe our commandments are universal (they don't necessarily apply to every CEO), exhaustive (there are others we could add) or perfectly balanced (some are more important or relevant than others). Neither, as it happens, are we in full agreement with all of them! But we believe they capture in a compact format what our co-authors and other CEOs say and think about nominating people to key jobs. Above all, they provide a good starting point for coaching.

The Idea to Take Away from Coaching Session 2
Nominating your key men and women is once again a matter of vision. You must look ahead and build a pipeline of talent while constantly viewing your people through a lens of intense scrutiny as they develop. Successful nomination is also all about rigorous selection processes (as opposed to "gut instinct"), a genuine interest in human beings and a commitment to learning. If you invest in the right people, they will repay you many times over.

6.3   COACHING SESSION 3: ENABLING

This time, let's start with some questions before we frame the issue. Do you agree with the following statements? Yes or no?

Ten Statements to Agree or Disagree With

1. A good CEO knows the business better than anybody else in the company.
2. A good CEO knows what will happen in the industry during the next decade.
3. A good CEO makes all the important decisions.
4. A good CEO allocates organisational resources and constantly monitors how effectively they are being used.
5. A good CEO tells her direct reports how to do their jobs.
6. A good CEO rewards outstanding performance.
7. A good CEO punishes underperformance.
8. A good CEO lives by her own rules.
9. A good CEO is always right.
10. Even if in the wrong, a good CEO never admits mistakes publicly.

If your reaction was to disagree with most of the statements, you have the mindset of an enabling leader, and you can skip the following two paragraphs. If you did not, read on.

Richard Rushton told us with conviction, "The days of the CEO who knows everything, makes every decision, exercises absolute control of the whole organisation are over." We agree wholeheartedly, although we note that the old style of management has lingered in some cultures and industries longer than in others. Today, even if it is not wholly eradicated, the 3Cs model of leadership under which the CEO made all major decisions ("command"), allocated resources and monitored performance ("control"), and rewarded and punished ("carrot and stick") is well and truly outdated. The final bastions fell under the onslaught of global competition.

The contemporary CEO cannot pretend he knows more than other members of the organisation, has access to data and information they don't and sees further ahead anyone else, because everyone knows that's not true. Today's knowledge workers have superior technical skills, and technology has made information accessible to all. In management, as in other fields, collaboration has long since replaced individual genius as the principal source of creativity. Trying to apply the old model is simply ineffective and inefficient. From "commander-in-chief" the CEO has become "chief enabler of the organisation." Her role is to *enable* other employees to perform.

Enabling leadership is grounded in different assumptions about followers' needs, abilities and values and leader-follower interaction than under the 3Cs model. Enabling leaders believe that the people they work with are adults (do not need parental guidance to make choices and can look after themselves) and professionals (are better than anybody else—including the CEO—at what they do, want to do a good a job and continue learning). Such employees don't need to be directed, just helped to perform at their best. Like professional athletes they do not need their goals and the ways to achieve them to be developed by a more senior person. They simply need assistance in mastering their own practices and achieving goals through the creation of a productive environment and emotional support. In short, business leadership has come to resemble coaching.

Shuzo Kaihori of Yokogawa Electric Company (Japan), who during his 40-year-plus career experienced his fair share of 3Cs leadership admits: "That's the biggest change in my career. In the past, I preferred to be more hands-on than to pass on the decision-making. But now a CEO has to let people decide themselves."

Enabling leadership is a complex construct with many facets, but in keeping with our co-authors' thinking, we will simplify rather than complicate it. In the following few pages we will describe a number of specific practices, which—in their view and ours—allow CEOs to play the enabling role effectively.

Reducing Uncertainty This core leadership practice becomes even more important at times of increasing complexity, which puts additional pressure on employees and may lead to stress and reduced performance. Our 20 CEOs mentioned some specific techniques:

- Setting clear vision, values, goals and expectations. Having only a few priorities, described in simple—and preferably quantitative—terms, radiates confidence.
- Distributing leadership throughout the organisation. Increasing the number of leaders at different levels, who in turn take on the role of reducing uncertainty for their followers.
- Streamlining organisational structure and governance. Having as few rules as possible. Avoiding the creation of new policies, procedures and instructions, unless absolutely necessary. Getting rid of outdated rules, regulations and procedures.

- Using simple language in conversations and company documents. Mentoring people to simplify rather than complicate things. Making people accountable for creating unnecessary complexity.
- Discontinuing outdated products, closing facilities and selling assets, which lost their strategic appeal, and letting go people who could no longer be productive.
- Promoting clarity and transparency at all organisational levels. Making information and data accessible and understandable to all members of the organisation. Or doing as Diego Bolzonello suggests: "I also think transparency, is very, very important, which is one reason that I work with open doors and receive people continuously."

Encouraging Collaboration and Removing Organisational Barriers Effective collective action is a cornerstone of corporate performance in today's world. Effective CEOs promote horizontal, vertical and diagonal collaboration in their companies by setting expectations, allocating time, establishing platforms and formats for collaborative work, and rewarding collaborative behaviour. They become chief facilitators of their organisations as they take on this new role of helping other people to perform collectively.

Good CEOs recognise that collaboration does not come naturally— and that modern organisations are full of objective and subjective barriers to it, such as asymmetrical knowledge, geographical distance, organisational hierarchy and even office design. Effective leaders spot these barriers and remove them. Most importantly they set an example of openness and proactivity in fostering collaboration. Diego Bolzonello repeats: "My doors are always open. It's a way of saying: 'We have no secrets and we're all going in the same direction.' There is no boundary between my office and other offices. It's very simple."

Creating Productive Autonomy for Employees From Peter Drucker, known as "the founder of modern management," we learned that knowledge workers need both headroom and elbowroom to be productive. Good CEOs create this autonomy by giving their people freedom to work the way they want and make their own decisions. Here's Diego Bolzonello again: "I think it would be absolutely wrong to have a slogan: 'Work this way!' We have to encourage people to work in whatever way helps us reach our objective."

The concept of "productive autonomy" applies both to individual performers and organisational units such as divisions, departments, factories and shops. Peter Coleman puts it this way: "Create an environment where they feel safe to take the actions and decisions when they need to."

According to our experts, effective CEOs should make as few decisions as possible, giving the opportunity instead to other people in the organisation. "The CEO has to take the *essential* decisions of the company, not substitute himself with his deputies," explains Jean Sentenac. A good rule is to look around and ask yourself, "Is there anyone (or any group) in the organisation who could take this decision?" Only if the answer is an affirmative "no" should the CEO go ahead and make the decision.

Giving Employees a Voice If you listen carefully to a truly outstanding CEO, you will hear more questions than statements, more silence than speech. You will hear not just "We want to go there" but "What do you think? Can we go there or not? Who agrees with this?" Such CEOs work with their people so that the decision is arrived at together. The practice of *fair leadership*—whereby everyone has an opportunity to contribute, every voice is heard, every idea is discussed and every decision is explained to all who will be touched by its consequences—is one of the pillars of effective leadership.

Supportive Challenging Enabled employees need to feel the CEO's support to perform well, but they should not be allowed to relax and become complacent. They need to strive constantly to become more effective, creative and productive. Good CEOs believe in the ability of their people and, as long as they prove effective, give them complete support. At the same time, they challenge their colleagues by questioning their assumptions, encouraging alternative thinking, negotiating higher targets and provoking unorthodox approaches. They energise their staff with ambitious goals, tough benchmarks and examples of superior performance—along with stories of hubris that led to disaster. Good CEOs push their employees to experiment, to take risks and to learn from failure.

Educating Enabling leaders (like Alex in our first coaching session) make learning available to every employee and turn it into one of the company's values. They build it into every job and create training programmes or corporate universities, rotating people across positions, functions and geographies to broaden their horizons. Under leaders like these, investment in employee development becomes the most protected line of the budget. The CEOs themselves take on the roles of educators, mentors and coaches and get their executives to do the same. "Leaders teaching future leaders" becomes an organisation-wide practice.

Staying in Touch with the Business and the Outside World Effective CEOs keep their hands off but their eyes on everything. They know what happens in and around the company by making deep dives: visiting back offices and shop floors, speaking with and serving customers, and directly calling on people at different levels of hierarchy. Enabling leaders are in a constant dialogue with the organisation, they listen more than tell ("at least two-thirds versus one-third" in the words of Vladimir Rashevsky) and they ask coaching-style questions to facilitate this dialogue.

Diego Bolzonello shared his best practices with us. "Next week, I'm going to the US," he said. "I will visit a few shops to understand how people walk inside and how the layout of the shoes works. It's important sometimes to go and understand. To make a decision you must know what you are doing. But the biggest mistake is to decide *against* your managers. They must trust you and trust that you understand the business." He adds: "You must also take care of complaints. If a manager complains, don't dismiss it as stupid. If it arrives in your office, it's never stupid!"

Good CEOs also monitor the "big picture" by constantly reviewing performance indicators, but most importantly proactively speaking with colleagues, consultants, experts, analysts, investors, academics and politicians.

Role Modelling This practice is as old as leadership itself, but several of our co-authors insist it's particularly relevant for enabling leadership. This is because it creates two important outcomes: first behaviour benchmarks for the followers and legitimacy for the leader. "Some CEOs think they are above the fundamental values and principles of the organisation," says Peter Coleman. "But you must set the benchmark for others. You are a role model and an enforcer."

How *Not* to Be an Enabling CEO

We don't like to be negative in our coaching sessions, but ultimately it's important to look at what you *mustn't* do, if you want to enable people effectively. And we received much good advice from our 20 CEOs:

- Peter Coleman starts with a very specific recommendation: "The CEO should never be seen yelling at employees and making them feel belittled."
- Diego Bolzonello suggests: "Making politics in the company is very dangerous. Preferring one person to another person is wrong. It's important to make links between people, rather than building barriers."
- "Never feel so successful that you isolate yourself," says Miguel Galuccio.
- "Don't put too much pressure on people and motivate them only with money," suggests Stefan Messer.
- "You must try to avoid any possible conflicts and tensions, between various groups," says Vladimir Rashevsky.

At this point, however, we feel there's some need for a reality check. Any reader who's ever worked in any kind of organisation or lived in any kind of family will know that, wherever there's more than one person, there's inevitably a conflict. "I mean, you must avoid *igniting* these sorts of situations," smiles Rashevsky, when challenged. "Essentially, as a person occupying a position of power your whole life is one big conflict!" "The most important thing is not to let conflicts among people grow. Otherwise, they'll grow and damage the company," explains Jean Sentenac.

Ultimately, it seems, modern leadership is earned rather than bestowed. Or as José Ángel Sánchez concludes: "You need leadership—not the kind that the company gives you when they name you as CEO. This is given to you. You need recognition by the organisation. Are your people motivated, well organised and dedicated to the job? Most of all, are you respected?"

Respected? Of course. But loved? That's something else altogether. You don't need love to enable your people. As Jeffrey Immelt says, "GE has more than 300,000 people. Some days they all hate me!"

The Idea to Take Away from Coaching Session 3
Leadership is not what it used to be. It's about *enabling people rather than issuing orders*. The enabling CEO tries to keep things simple and fight organisational complexity in all its forms. He or she makes as few decisions as possible, doesn't meddle in office politics or power struggles and challenges staff, by setting high standards and asking tough questions. In return, such leaders support their followers with resources, attention and mentoring—energising the whole organisation. The emotional acumen that we encountered in Class 5 plays a major role, but newer forms of communication, such as Twitter, town hall sessions and "management by walking around," are continuing to change the role of the enabling CEO as we write.

6.4   Coaching Session 4: Managing Crises

We'll start our final coaching session with a story (this time involving one of our 20 CEOs) and leave it to you reflect on it, before concluding with some feedback of our own.

Crisis in the Gulf: A Dramatic Tale of Two CEOs in Three Acts

Act I: April 2010
Some 40 miles off the Louisiana coast stands the Deepwater Horizon drilling rig, chartered by global oil company, BP, from owner and operator, Transocean. At 9.45 pm on 20 April, the mobile, floating facility is ripped apart by a huge explosion. Of the 126 crew members on board, 17 are injured and 11 are declared missing. Two days later, the rig sinks, and oil starts to spread across the Gulf of Mexico. Eventually, satellite images will show the slick affecting 180,000 km² of ocean. The environmental and human impact will be less easy to measure.

Act II: May and June 2010
BP's British CEO, Tony Hayward, initially downplays the oil spill. But, a month after the explosion, with the slick still spreading, he concedes that BP "made a few little mistakes early on" in dealing with local fishermen and—shortly afterwards—that there is an "environmental catastrophe" in the Gulf of Mexico. He famously takes a

(continued)

(continued)

day off to attend a yacht race in England and, in a moment of stress, tells reporters, "I'd like my life back."

On 23 June, Bob Dudley, a managing director of BP, is put in charge of BP's Gulf Coast restoration operations—taking over day-to-day crisis management from Hayward. He is responsible not only for the clean-up but also for liaison with the authorities and the public. Dudley grew up in Mississippi and has worked in the oil business since completing his MBA—and for BP since 1999, when the company took over Amoco. He is known for his calm, flexibility and diplomacy in difficult situations.

Dudley delivers the message that BP will do its duty and pay for the damage caused calmly and clearly. He does not show impatience or frustration.

Act III: July 2010 onwards
Dudley's bridge building is beginning to make an impact. At the end of July, BP announces that he will take over as CEO from October. Under Dudley's leadership, the company will go on to plead guilty to 11 felony counts of manslaughter and one of lying to Congress, as well as paying out more than $4.5 billion. However, over the coming years he will turn the company's fortunes and reputation around. In 2016, a Hollywood movie is made about the disaster and its aftermath. Dudley, who is still in charge, is *not* one of the characters.

Look in any dictionary, and you'll see that the word crisis has its roots in the Greek "krísis" or "decision." And yet, in times of crisis all the usual mechanisms for decision-making break down. The equilibrium that existed beforehand disappears, and the level of uncertainty shoots sky high. Algorithms, heuristics, rules and procedures that used to deliver good decisions become irrelevant, if not counterproductive. The situation calls for a break with the past and entirely new solutions.

From a psychological perspective, crisis-induced stress leads to a reduction in people's cognitive abilities. Their "human" brain switches off, and their "animal' brain kicks in. To different degrees they stop thinking rationally, and subconscious mechanisms of defence are activated: most commonly, denial, procrastination, activism and/or scapegoating. At times of crisis humans look for guidance, protection and assistance. In short, the need for leadership increases dramatically. People are actively looking for a saviour who can offer ready-made solutions. The only trouble is, CEOs are human beings too.

As we saw from the story above, leaders may also stop thinking and acting rationally. They're programmed to fall victim to denial, just like the rest of us. Yet the fact of being chief executive officers puts them centre stage at times of crisis. They can't stay behind the scenes and direct others from the wings. They have no choice other than to step into the spotlight and execute.

By definition crisis is an abnormal event, something that happens against the expectations and the will of the CEO. Yet in today's volatile and turbulent world, the frequency of such events is increasing dramatically. Every twenty-first-century CEO will face many crises during her shrinking tenure. Navigating the company through such moments is the task which no one but the CEO can accomplish—and which requires certain attitudes, skills and preparation. That's why our 20 co-authors consider crisis management one of their key roles and offer some specific advice on how to go about playing it.

Acceptance and Preparation Good CEOs know for sure that they will have to live through a crisis, which could be caused by external or internal factors. As Jeffrey Immelt points out: "Anybody that has been around in last 10 or 20 years has seen what I would call 'tera-risks'—from outside the company. In other words, the global financial crisis, 9/11, Fukushima nuclear power plant, you know, oil spills, stuff like that."

All the same, it's important to know something about where the next crisis may come from—and to work on expanding this knowledge. This holds true for all sectors, but it's absolutely fundamental in some, such as oil and gas. "There is an enormous range of uncertainties in our industry," says Renato Bertani. "There are geological risks, uncertainties on well productivity, on the reservoir, on the cost, on the market, on the process, on the geopolitical situation. So we need to prepare to live with the uncertainties." Preparation means working out scenarios for organisational response, training people and accumulating resources that critical for business survival. Good CEOs study what others have done and spread this knowledge throughout the organisation.

On the other hand, even good CEOs don't know when a crisis will strike. But by assuming it's inevitable, openly talking about it and preparing for it, they reduce its exceptionality and move it to the category of "normal" events, making it easier for everyone in the organisation to cope when the worst happens.

Risk Mitigation According to our experts the best way to manage crisis is to avoid one. For them risk mitigation is just another part of the CEO's job. "Analysing the risk—identifying the risk first and then controlling it, managing it—is... another skill that I believe it is very important for a CEO," says Mazen Ahmed Khayyat of El-Khayyat Group (Saudi Arabia). Good CEOs develop a comprehensive system of risk identification and mitigation, which combines mathematical tools, big data, diverse human expertise and leadership judgement grounded in experience, knowledge and intelligence (particularly the systemic thinking that we saw in Class 5).

"The key is trying to figure out how to set the odds in your favour," says Renato Bertani. "That's the big difference from gambling. There, the odds are in favour of the casino. In our business you want to understand sufficiently so that most of the time we win."

Cool Headedness When the crisis eventually strikes, the most important task for the CEO is to overcome the natural human tendency to become reactive and descend to subconscious defences. Good CEOs keep a cool head and continue to work rationally, relying particularly on their ability to think systemically. As Vladimir Rashevsky points out, "It's important to have a certain ability to work under pressure in an unexpected or crisis situation. Creative thinking in general—and especially under stress—is definitely an asset. In smaller companies, stress-resilience may be even more important for a CEO to succeed than strategic vision."

Contrary to the widespread myth, effective CEOs do not rush to act in times of crisis but instead analyse the new reality, adjust their mental models, evaluate options, make a decision and only then act. The difference with times of normality is that they must do all this quickly. As Diego Bolzonello says: "You have to solve the problem...very fast, very quickly."

Agility A cool head and speedy action are essential for resolving a crisis. Flexibility, quick reactions to initial feedback, swift adjustments to the course of action (if necessary)... these are the ingredients of effective crisis management. None of our experts used the term "agile," but they spoke about everything it implies: short feedback loops, experimentation, adjustments, learning from mistakes. As another CEO (not from our sample of 20) once told us, "To manage in crisis you need to be like a cat: super attentive to the environment, scanning it constantly for the new signs of danger or hope, and moving around with your legs half-bent, so you can jump away quickly."

"Teaming" Although the CEO may take on the lion's share of responsibility for crisis management, the dramatic nature of the situation does not change the fundamental feature of today's business landscape: complexity. After all, no one can manage a company single-handed in "normal" times of predictability and stability. So, when things turn uncertain, it becomes even more important to draw on the intelligence and experience of many people. Effective CEOs organise what Harvard professor Amy Edmondson calls "teaming": collaboration that cuts across formal organisational boundaries. If you like, it's teamwork "on the fly"—designed to mobilise the creative energy of people from different parts of company and achieve the ultimate goal, which is not only to overcome crisis but also to come out of it stronger than before.

Attention to People At times of crisis effective business leaders must become even more attentive to the ideas and feelings of their employees. Through "teaming," CEOs seek out solutions and test them. In return, they provide the direction and authority that their staff seek. But they also need to supply empathy and sympathy for the challenges afoot. Good CEOs demonstrate this human touch by acknowledging the unprecedented nature of the situation and changing working conditions. They make themselves more available to the organisation, providing support and advice—and communicating with warmth and humour. Above all, they exhibit optimism and confidence that—by working together—the crisis can be tamed.

Here's some final advice from Jeffrey Immelt:

Over the last 15 years I became better at risk management. I understand a bit more about what could happen in the world. When I first became CEO, I knew what I wanted to do, but I didn't have two or three contingencies in case it didn't work. Maybe it's not the door straight ahead you need to open. You could go around the sides and find different ways to get what you want done.

The Idea to Take Away from Coaching Session 4
Don't make a drama out of a crisis. Accept that risk-taking is an indispensable part of your role and *prepare yourself mentally and physically for some degree of crisis management* at some point in your career. Keep your feet on the ground and be ready to roll up your sleeves at any moment. Mentally rehearse a different behaviour pattern and quickly switch mode, when unexpected (but not, we hope, entirely unforeseen) circumstances arise.

To sum up our journey through four coaching sessions, while the business world is undoubtedly more complex than ever before, the work of the CEO may be simpler than its portrayal by leadership experts implies. Following our conversations with 20 global CEOs, we believe that in essence it can be reduced to four key roles: envisioning, nominating, enabling and crisis management. But, as we've seen in the course of this class, "simple" certainly doesn't mean "easy." If you're a prospective or even current CEO, we only hope that our coaching has given you some ideas and inspiration to rise to the many challenges ahead.

SOME FURTHER READING

Bass, B. (1990) Bass & Stogdill Handbook of leadership: theory, research, and managerial application. 3rd edition. The Free Press.
Bennis, W. G. (2009). On Becoming a Leader. 4th Edition. Philadelphia: Basic Books.
Chong, J. K. (2004) Six steps to better crisis management. Journal of Business Strategy, Vol. 25 (3).
Finkelstein, S. & Hambrick, D. C. (1996) Strategic Leadership: Top Executives and Their Effects on Organizations. West Publishing Company.
Garten, J. E (2000) The Mind of the CEO, Basic Books, New York.
Murray, K. (2017) People with Purpose: How Great Leaders Use Purpose to Build Thriving Organizations. Kogan Page Publishers.
Porter, M. E. & Nitin, N. (2006) What Is Leadership: The CEO's Role in Large, Complex Organizations. In Handbook of Leadership Theory and Practice. Edited by N. Nohria and K. Khurana. Harvard Business School Publishing.
Rotemberg, J. & Saloner, G. (1998) Visionaries, Managers, and Strategic Direction. Harvard Business School.
Smits, J. S. & Ally, N. Z. (2003) "Thinking The Unthinkable"—Leadership's Role In Creating Behavioral Readiness For Crisis Management. Competitiveness Review: An International Business Journal, Vol. 13 (1).

CHAPTER 7

Class 7: Style—Five Ways to Project Yourself as a CEO

Abstract After six intensive classes, it should be fairly clear what makes a successful CEO. But there's something intangible that we haven't yet conveyed. It's what we felt in the presence of our school of 20 global business leaders, as much as anything they actually said to us: a matter of style rather than substance. One thing that was fairly clear from the first interview onwards is that our CEOs champion their company at all times. But that certainly didn't stop them from taking an active interest in our conversation and our own organisations. In fact this was (paradoxically, perhaps) what made them so interesting and compelling to talk to. Another factor was that they weren't prevented by cultural differences from finding common ground with us, thanks to their global mindset. Finally, as confirmed by our questioning, they came across as fit and healthy, most of them actively practising sports or hobbies that enable them to achieve a balanced lifestyle.

Keywords Company champion • Compassion • Discipline • Global mindset • Healthy lifestyle

Al que mucho se le confía, mucho se le exige. (Spain)
Meaning: From everybody to whom much is given, much is expected.

ಆರೋಗ್ಯವೇ ಭಾ *(India)*
Meaning: Health is wealth.

© The Author(s) 2018   109
S. Shekshnia et al., *CEO School*,
https://doi.org/10.1007/978-981-10-7865-1_7

忙中閑あり *(Japan)*
Meaning: Even when you're very busy, there's occasionally time to take a rest.

An Opening Poem: The Formula for CEO
What are CEOs made of?
Not slugs or snails, or puppy dogs' tails
Nor sugar and spice and all things nice.
*So what **are** CEOs made of?*
Traits, experience and education,
Skills, roles: like vision and nomination,
An enabler rather than a master,
A safe pair of hands in a disaster.
But that's not all CEOs are made of...

After six intensive classes, you should have a pretty good idea of what makes a successful CEO. To remind you, they're summed up (in verse) above. But there's something else—something more intangible—that we haven't yet been able to convey. It's what we *felt* in the presence of our school of 20 global business leaders as much as what they actually said to us: a matter of style as much as substance or content. In other words, there's a *je ne sais quoi* aura given off by CEOs, which—as good researchers—we'll nonetheless attempt to explain.

Looking back over our research project, the process of conducting the 20 interviews was harder than we thought it would be. Identifying suitable candidates, getting their agreement, researching their careers and fitting meetings into our own busy schedules all added up to a major organisational challenge. If we're to be completely honest, it turned into something of a chore at times. Yet, as soon as we were in the presence of our CEOs, we found ourselves re-energised.

After each encounter, still buzzing from the conversational reinvigoration, we asked ourselves the same question: would I like to work for this person? And each time we gave the same answer: yes. In short, most of our CEOs cast something of a spell on us.

Take, for example, Vladimir Rashevsky of SUEK (Russia). At first glance, he does not come across as a social wizard. Very tall, serious and rather pale, he looks like an intellectual, more than a business leader. But when he starts talking, everything changes. His smile lights up not just his face but the entire room. He radiates warmth in the way he speaks and listens. And his body language, though not extravagant, is strikingly effective. He leans forward and makes eye contact, filling the space between him and us with physical presence.

The easy option would be to dismiss this phenomenon as a simple, irreducible concept like "charisma," originally introduced by the German sociologist, Max Weber (1864–1920). It's a term that's particularly popular among journalists in search of a synonym for "leadership qualities." But in academic circles charisma is extremely out-of-date, perhaps because it's hard to measure and impossible to develop.

If you want to understand why we object to it so much, just read what Weber had to say: "Charisma is a certain quality of an individual by virtue of which he is set apart from ordinary men and treated as endowed with supernatural, superhuman, or at least exceptional powers or qualities." And it gets worse. According to Weber, these powers are: "not accessible to the ordinary person, but are regarded as of divine origin... and, on the basis of them the individual concerned is treated as a leader."

Although one or two academics have tried to reinstate and redefine the concept of charisma for the modern age, for us it remains vague and unmeasurable... verging on the unsound and even dangerous. Others appeal instead to less fanciful notions like "gravitas" or "presence," but these are equally ill defined. And we're not sure that they always apply in a new age of leadership where enabling other people to lead has become a paradigm.

Instead of relying on such fuzzy notions, we prefer to analyse our impressions of our 20 co-authors into several key components of CEO style—which is what we attempt to do in this chapter.

You might remember that we started down this track, right at the beginning of our School of CEOs, when we identified passion as a personality trait that all our interviewees shared. And indeed, passion is probably part of the "magic" that we're talking about now, as well as curiosity (also highlighted in Class 2). But there are other ingredients: things you can actually *do* rather than a personality trait (or a mysterious aura) that you simply *have*.

7.1   CHAMPION YOUR COMPANY AT ALL TIMES

Every interview we did turned out to be unique, even though we were careful to put exactly the same set of seven questions about the essence of the CEO job to all of our co-authors. But we couldn't help noticing that everyone skilfully turned the conversation around to give concrete examples from their own companies. Most of them cleverly used the encounters to do a little networking or to exchange ideas about doing business in France, the Balkans or Russia. A few even offered to show us around their organisation's facilities or plants at a later date. When we met Yang Wansheng of China Machinery Engineering Corporation by video link, he kindly invited us to China: "We would like to see you in our head office just to show you our methods and their way of work."

Now, in other circumstances, this might be annoying—a bit like being cornered by people at parties who only want to talk about themselves. But pretty early in the process, it became clear that our CEOs were definitely not revealing much about their innermost selves, let alone their private lives and families. What they talked about at every possible opportunity was their *companies*—in terms of both their visions for the future and their achievements to date.

Some were very subtle about this, like Lee Chul-Kyoon of Daelim Industrial Co., Ltd. (South Korea). "I think that you have already acquired information about our company...," he stated but with an audible question mark, which gave him the opportunity to tell us about the history and global operations of this vast conglomerate, before the interview got underway.

Others, like Stefan Messer of Messer Group (Germany), unashamedly filled their answers to our questions with examples from their own organisation and its history. In fact, Messer confessed to "identifying" completely with the company. "It's much better than being in the background and taking the money to buy a boat or go on holiday all the time!" he laughed, contrasting himself with the stereotype of the worst kind of business tycoon.

However, having spoken to some 17 CEOs who are *not* owners or founders of their company, we believe this attitude is more widespread than Messer might think. Temel Kotil of Turkish Airlines had even more anecdotes about his organisation than our German representative—sometimes bombarding us with facts and stories before we could get our questions in edgeways. "This is not my own business actually," he stops to explain at one point. "They just pay me to work here. But I *feel* like this is my own business. It's very simple. If just one passenger is disappointed, I feel very bad."

As Jeff Immelt of General Electric (USA) said when we talked about the things a CEO should not do, "To lie, steal, those things are obvious, but I think the CEO can never put himself in front of the company. I am only about GE. I'm not a person separate from it. Everyone outside GE who knows me also knows that I put the company first. And I always say that people inside GE can question my decisions from time to time, but they can never question my intentions."

Do you really have to go so far as to identify with your organisation and put it first at all times? We're not so sure. Jean Sentenac of Axens (France) mentioned something that seems more important: "For me, being a CEO, first of all, is a spirit that person has to have for the good of a company in the short and long term."

As well as being the keeper of the company spirit, the CEO is also the organisation's storyteller. "Behind every successful company, there is a story," says Diego Bolzonello of Geox (Italy). "It's the evolution of the company that makes it seem different from other companies." As leader of the continued evolution, as we saw in the Class 6, you need clear vision for the future, but you shouldn't lose forget the present and the past, especially when you're talking to people outside the organisation. If you're in any doubt, just listen to José Ángel Sánchez of Real Madrid (Spain):

> The way things have moved for the club since the year 2000 until today is incredible. The club was not even in the top 20 of the most profitable clubs in the world in 2000, and now it's been in the number one position for the last five or six years. It was really a revolution. This was the most incredible thing: it's like being the first person who touched the Moon.

If you see your company in this way and then say it—without using the words "I," "me" or "my"—you don't need superpowers. Or rocket science.

7.2   BE INTERESTING BY BEING *INTERESTED*

Although our interviewees never lost an opportunity to champion their own companies, we were also very aware of them putting questions to us about our own business. Again, this didn't come across as nosy or inappropriate but charming and friendly. Nor was it a tactic to avoid answering difficult questions. On the contrary, they seemed to positively *enjoy* our conversations.

"I like these kinds of talks," said Yang Wansheng out loud. "It's very important, especially for the highest level of management to talk and collaborate in this way." Similarly, at one point in our exchange, Richard Rushton of Distell (South Africa) commented, unprompted: "You do ask interesting questions." In fact every single one of our 20 CEOs appeared fully engaged in our conversations at all times, helping us to clarify our questions and elaborating on their answers without being asked to. In short, they were—or at least gave the impression of being—*interested*.

Of course, we find our questions interesting too, but that's not the point. What's important here is that by demonstrating interest, the 20 CEOs became more interest*ing* to spend time with—and their comments seemed more worthy of note. What's more, we found ourselves not simply recording their answers but warming to them as people and respecting them as leaders.

Psychologists who have carried out research into this phenomenon have identified exactly the same factors. Truly magnetic personalities are not those who loudly command the attention of an entire room but those who are able to make others feel like the most important person in that room. To put it another way, the best way to be interesting is to be interested. And people are more likely to follow a leader who makes them feel important. It's obvious, when you stop to think about it. Whoever heard of a successful leader who was boring and inattentive? But, curiously, "being interested" is never listed in a job description, performance appraisal form or 360-degree assessment exercise. It's so fundamental that it never becomes explicit—and therefore risks being forgotten by aspiring CEOs.

Jean Sentenac came close to articulating the link between being interesting and being interested, at the end of our conversation—in one of those "doorknob" moments that all interviewers (and therapists) know so well, when a probing issue is broached at the very last minute. "I think it is important to be interesting as a person," he said. "If we meet, I would like to know about you, to be able to socialise with you outside the business itself. I like to talk to people, get to know them better… and let them know me better."

We pressed him on it a little. Can those who are not naturally inquisitive about other people learn a few formulaic questions so as to appear more interested? Or would that come across as fake? "I would not say it's something to work on. It has to be natural," he concluded. However, on a purely organisational level, engaging with others or making a little time to socialise is something that can be factored in. "Sometimes it's difficult to maintain because of time pressure," said Sentenac, "but we can use our travelling and personal time, always trying to keep our eyes open."

"It's also a way to be in the community network," added Sentenac finally, confirming that there are many practical benefits to this attitude, as well as intangibles. Who knows whether the person sitting next to you on the airplane or across the table at a dinner party is going to turn into a valuable business contact?

The other practical benefit of growing "human antennae" is that they help you to keep abreast of the latest trends—all the more important as the pace of technological and social change accelerates. "Take a lot of interest to understand what your son or daughter is interested in and why," advises Diego Bolzonello. "What's the phenomenon that's catching them? What's the music that's changing? It's very important to keep up with the times. We need to understand evolution over time for our business—and that's made by culture."

7.3   DEVELOP A GLOBAL MINDSET

Bolzonello was talking about popular culture not industry or *national* culture, of course. But this was an issue we were acutely aware of in the course of carrying out our research. We interviewed business leaders from every continent, every major world religion and a wide spread of industries. Yet, despite their local differences, they all had one thing in a common: a *global* mindset. They spoke about the world as if it was a single place—interconnected rather than fragmented into individual regions or countries. They talked about globalisation as an opportunity rather than a threat, diversity as an asset rather than a source of problems. And though, by definition, only one of our interviews was really with someone from our own culture, in 100% of our encounters, we were made to feel at home by the CEOs. It wasn't so much that they (or we) are cultural chameleons or global citizens. It was simply that they (and hopefully we) have a global mindset: a fully integrated worldview.

This is partly, of course, down to the necessity of twenty-first-century business. Today, some might say, there is no choice other than to adjust your attitude and extend your horizons. "You have to understand globalisation, the intersection of global markets," as Jeffrey Immelt expressed it. This is an extension of the systemic and holistic thinking we saw in Class 5, but here the "big picture" is not your company, your industry or even your national economy but the entire planet as a one enormous, interconnected market.

To be truly successful as a business leader in this context, it helps if you can "develop yourself to successfully operate across different cultural boundaries and groups"—in the words of Peter Coleman of Woodside (Australia). Coleman has achieved this by working in global corporations and a variety of countries, including Indonesia and Nigeria, which—in many ways—could not be more culturally different from his native land. Most African and Asian businesses are still very formal and hierarchical, while Australia is famous for its easy-going, flat organisations.

Richard Rushton has had a similar career trajectory. "I've personally had the enormous advantage of having CEO roles on three different continents around the world: in Africa, on the Indian subcontinent and in South America," he says. "The ability to culturally connect with others across the globe is incredibly important for a CEO in a globally interconnected, changing world."

But what about business leaders who haven't had an international career in a global corporation? They clearly don't need the same kind of cultural compass as a Peter Coleman or a Richard Rushton. So do they really need to develop a global mindset? Nishi Vasudeva of Hindustan Petroleum (India) seemed mildly amused when we asked her (at an event in Moscow) how being a CEO in India differed from being a CEO elsewhere. "Honestly, I don't know!" she said. And yet, despite spending her entire career in India, she seemed perfectly at home in an international forum and comfortable dealing with people from all parts of the world. Maybe it's simply because she could see the connections between these parts so clearly.

Richard Rushton perhaps put his finger on what we could see in Vasudeva and all of our other interviewees. "The CEO is accountable for making sense of the world we are living in," he said. "It's a 'fourth dimension' that's becoming increasingly important, not just because we're living in an increasingly interconnected world but because of global volatility. Somehow the CEO needs to make sense of this constant change for the organisation."

In other words, a global mindset can have local benefit. To take Rushton's own example, "South Africa faces many issues with its own political and economic dynamics. All of that requires a CEO to be a quick reader of events: geopolitical, social and otherwise."

Similarly, Didie Soewondho of PT Wijaya Infrastruktur (Indonesia) insists on the importance of "knowledge about government relations that might affect the company, particularly law and regulation, and including political influence." He also speaks about the need for CEOs to understand "green, environmental and sustainable development trends." This is a "global mindset" on a different scale—seeing your company as part of a system that includes the planet itself. The idea is echoed by Yang Wansheng: "We emphasise the protection of the planet and the natural environment. And then we must see our results and our success in the whole world. When we see that, then we can make the conclusion if we are successful CEOs or not."

Working at INSEAD, probably the world's most global business school, we know exactly what he means. Many students apply to the institution, simply because they intend to have an international career, but when they arrive they find they are getting something much more powerful, that is, the ability to see the world from multiple different perspectives all at once. They think they're buying a cultural compass, but instead their brain is being rewired to see global business as a single system—and business as a force for good on the planet and its people. As Shuzo Kaihori of Yokogawa (Japan)—another CEO with a single-company, single-country career—says, "Exposure to a different world, different people is *always* a good thing." Personally, we'd go so far as to say that it's the best way to develop a global mindset.

7.4   STAY FIT AND HEALTHY

Kaihori was in his mid-sixties when we interviewed him and was approaching the end of his term as CEO and he looked slim, fit and energetic. We asked him his secret. "I play a little golf," he laughed. "In the past I rode a motorbike, but after I was nominated as President I said: No, it's too risky!"

It was similar story with the other 19 CEOs. Nearly all of them were in their fifties or older, but they were in great physical shape. Nor was this an illusion created by well-tailored suits and expensive ties. They had a positive personal image and knew how to project it—and left us with an impression of energetic, elegant and attractive people.

At this point, we must stress that none of these people are friends of ours. Nor have we anything to gain from flattering their egos. We are simply stating the facts. And though our sample may not be a representative cross-section of the world's CEOs, there is some highly statistical research to suggest that good-looking people are better at getting jobs than the aesthetically challenged. No surprises there. But some studies go so far as to show that attractive CEOs receive higher compensation and even that their companies achieve higher profits.

Again, it all makes sense when you think about it. Today's ideals of beauty tend to correlate "good-looking" with "healthy-looking." And it would be impossible to survive the gruelling lifestyle of a CEO without being physically fit. "It's important to keep in good physical shape," Jean Sentenac told us. "You have to pay attention to what you eat, drinking must be under control and to do sport is very important. With all the travelling and stress, you just have to be in good physical condition. It's part of the job. If you wake up tired, it will not be a good day. I've seen that for myself."

Doing sport is as much about fitness of mind as fitness of body. "Find a time to connect with family, friends and to have some social activity, hobby or sport, so as not to be consumed by the role of CEO," advises Richard Rushton. He, like many, is a golfer. "Even if I don't play for a few months because of work pressures," he continues. "I always find time to exercise between three and five times a week: running or cycling. It's extremely rewarding and important, because those activities relieve stress, give time for thinking."

Renato Bertani of Barra Energia (Brazil), though less of an exercise nut, insists on the importance of finding an activity to help you relax at weekends. "Life is not only about working," he insists. "Life is having a family, travelling, doing a hobby. I am a great fisherman. I fish every weekend when I have time. You have such a busy week and then comes Saturday and you are so exhausted and sometimes stressed. If you can spend a few hours doing something, it's so relaxing and on Monday, you are back to work and you are again very productive."

In the end, how you strike this balance in life is up to you. Shuzo Kaihori points out, "Japanese people are known for being addicted to work, but maybe it's just our working hours, not necessarily concentrated work time. It depends on each person how to achieve the balance of work and life. No one can guide you on your best balance. You have to judge for yourself." We believe that every CEO we spoke to—whether by focusing on sport, family, socialising, hobbies or reading—had not only found that balance but visibly radiated wellbeing as part of their personal style.

7.5   BE ORGANISED AND DISCIPLINED

During our interviews, we noticed several other elements of CEO style. We were struck by all our interviewees' evident intelligence, for example, but we were particularly bowled over by their high degree of organisational discipline. The truth is that you can't be effective as a CEO without ruthless organisation. There are so many competing demands that you simply can't survive without rigorous systems and scheduling. Richard Rushton confirms it: "The ability to prioritise work and efforts is an incredibly important skill, which is why I think academic institutions play such a significant role in helping to groom and polish potential CEOs." As we saw in Class 3, the curriculum at university is often less important than the life skills it inculcates—organisation and discipline being a prime example.

There is clearly a balance to be struck between reaction and reflection, but most CEOs we know manage to operate a "rapid-response" system while at the same time disciplining themselves to shut off distractions. "I continuously answer emails," says Diego Bolzonello. "If they ask me I answer them immediately." But at the same time, he says half his job is "organisation, numbers, strategic points." You have to be an extraordinary time manager (as well as having an excellent personal assistant), if you're going to make this work.

As Nishi Vasudeva points out, you cannot expect those who work for you to be organised unless you demonstrate discipline yourself: "One thing that is very important in terms of integrity is a sense that, if you say this is the way things should be done, then you should also do things in that way yourself. It's not about saying, 'I want discipline, I want this, I want that'. It's about 'walking the talk' and not expecting any special treatment. The integrity of your words and actions should be very clear."

Ultimately too, it's a matter of self-confidence as well as integrity. You need to be disciplined if you're going to believe in yourself. "You've got to be extremely demanding on yourself," says Jeffrey Immelt. "You have to be a self-starter so that you can look in the mirror every day and be critical yet at the same time know yourself and be self-confident again."

If you want any further proof that CEOs are a disciplined breed, consider that all but one of our interviews started—and finished—on time.

While they were talking, our interviewees maintained their concentration. They made sure not to be disturbed by phone calls or distracted by emails. Our hunch is that, once we were out of the room, they became entirely absorbed in their next new task, but that remains a matter for speculation, so we'll settle for summing up our observations.

7.6   THE LAST MAGIC INGREDIENT OF CEO SUCCESS

Throughout the chapters of this book, we have attempted to distil the essence of CEO success and to bottle them in our pages. In this class, we've focused on CEO style, with more of an emphasis on what we observed rather than what we were told. And we think this style has four main ingredients: being a standard-bearer for the company; taking a genuine interest in other people; developing a global mindset; maintaining a healthy, balanced way of life; and applying an iron discipline to organising yourself.

But of course, there is no such thing as a magic potion in real life. Even if you apply all the learning from our *CEO School*, there are no guarantees that you will make it to the top—let alone have a long and high-performing tenure (which will be the subject of our next and final class). "I have been *lucky* in life," Renato Bertani told us. And he wasn't the only one of our 20 interviewees to make this admission. Of course, as golfer, Gary Player

---

A Closing Poem: The Magic Ingredients of a CEO
Eye of newt and toe of frog,
Wool of bat and tongue of dog...
Al ingredients of Shakespeare's potion.
*But **our** spell has a different notion.*
Fluxweed, knotgrass and hind parts of rat?
Wolfsbane, asphodel and hair of cat?
No, that is Harry Potter's spelling
CEO style is more compelling:
Company champion, global thinking,
Interested means interesting,
Healthy lifestyle and disciplined mind.
But that's not all you will need to find.
The magic required not to get stuck
In your career – of course, it's luck!

famously said, "The harder I practise, the luckier I get." As it is in golf, so it is in business. There is always the chance of a freak gust of wind that will work in your favour.

SOME FURTHER READING

Aurelius, Marcus (2006) Meditations. Penguin Classics.

Bates, S. (2016) Discover your CEO Brand. McGraw-Hill.

Garten, J. E. (2000) The Mind of the CEO, Basic Books, New York.

Loeher, J., Schwarz, T. (2005) The Power of Full Engagement: Managing Energy, Not Time, Is the Key to High Performance and Personal Renewal. Free Press.

Maak, T., Pless, K., Voegtlin, N., Business (2016) Statesman or Shareholder Advocate? CEO Responsible Leadership Styles and the Micro-Foundations of Political CSR. Journal of Management Studies, Volume 53, Issue 3, p. 463–493.

Murphy, M. (2016). Leadership Styles Are Often Why CEOs Get Fired. https://www.forbes.com/sites/markmurphy/2015/07/16/leadership-styles-are-often-why-ceos-get-fired

Murray, K. (2017) People with Purpose: How Great Leaders Use Purpose to Build Thriving Organizations. Kogan Page Publishers.

Murray, K. (2011) Communicate to Inspire: A Guide for Leaders. Kogan Page Publishers.

Newport, C. (2016) Deep Work: Rules for Focused Success in a Distracted World. Grand Central Publishing.

Preston, T. (2001) The President and His Inner Circle: Leadership Style and the Advisory Process in Foreign Affairs, Columbia University Press.

Sandling, J. (2015) Leading with Style: The Comprehensive Guide to Leadership Styles.

Sperry, L. (2008) Effective Leadership: Strategies for Maximizing Executive Productivity and Health. Brunner-Routledge, N.Y.

The Arbinder Institute (2002) Leadership and Self-Deception: Getting Out of the Box. Berrett-Koehler Publishers.

Class 8: Staying at the Top (But Not Too Long)—The Five Challenges All CEOs Must Master

Abstract In this chapter we have come full circle as our focus turns once again to the question: what makes a good CEO? However, this time, we are looking at it from the point of view of the CEO legacy.

Business bosses need to recognise and deal effectively with challenges of loneliness and keeping in touch with reality. We recommend that CEOs stay long enough (seven to ten years) to deliver a sustainable return to shareholders and beat the competition, continuing to learn so as not to become stale all the while. However, they should also leave "on time" with the company in far better shape than when they started. And an essential part of this is preparing and selecting a successor.

Keywords CEO tenure • Loneliness • Sense of reality • Succession planning • Successor

Old age does not announce itself. (South Africa)

The devil places a pillow for a drunken man to fall upon. (Canada)

Una puerta está cerrada pero mil están abiertas. (Argentina)
Meaning: One door is shut but a thousand are open.

There are plenty of jokes about accountants and lawyers, but not many about CEOs. Indeed there may only be one. Here it is....

S. SHEKSHNIA ET AL.

It's No Joke Being a CEO
A large corporation had just hired a new CEO. Before he started the job, he was invited to a private meeting with the old CEO, who handed him three numbered envelopes. "Open them—in order— each time you hit a bad patch," she said.

Well, the first six months passed like a dream, but then, inexplicably, sales fell off a cliff. Sitting at his desk with his head in his hands after a particularly hard board meeting, the CEO suddenly remembered the envelopes. He took the first one out of his drawer and read the message: "Blame me." So the CEO called a press conference and told the world that the plummeting performance was all the fault of his predecessor.

To his surprise, the advice worked perfectly. Sales picked up again and everything went well for a year or so. Then there was a serious problem with one of the products and revenues started to decline alarmingly. This time the CEO went straight to the second envelope, which contained only one word: "Reorganise."

Again, the CEO did as he was advised. He hired some consultants, fired some staff, restructured and divested. Both markets and customers seemed pleased. But after several profitable quarters, the sales figures were heading south again and kept on falling. The board was making nasty noises, but the CEO wasn't worried, because he had one last envelope to save him. He went into his office, closed the door, sat down and opened it. The message read: "Prepare three envelopes."

Suffice to say, neither of the two leaders in this joke can be described as a success. As we discovered before we even started CEO School, you are only as good as your results. As an incoming CEO, you should be aiming for many years of beating the competition and generating sustainable returns for shareholders—not three envelopes, even if they are stuffed with substance (Classes 2 to 6), style (Class 7) and luck (which you won't get from any class). Be warned too that luck has its limits. It may save you for a year or two but is highly unlikely to hold out for a decade.

So, do our 20 CEOs have any final words of wisdom to keep you in the corner office/chauffeur-driven limo/corporate jet (delete as applicable)?

Miguel Galuccio (Argentina, YPF) shrugs his shoulders. "If you arrive in the CEO position and you survive, that makes you qualified to be in the seat," he says with an enigmatic smile.

Just make sure you don't sit there for too many hours a day, though! Or, as Richard Rushton (South Africa, Distell) puts it: "The CEO who sits behind a desk for 18 hours a day is unlikely to be successful." His point this time is not about achieving a healthy balance in life (as we saw in Class 7), so much as a warning that the CEO should never become cut off. "It's important that you never feel so successful that you isolate yourself," explains Galuccio, when pressed for further analysis.

8.1   Challenge 1: Keeping in Touch with Reality

Staying connected doesn't necessarily involve trendy leadership techniques of "management by walking around" or gimmicks like "suggestion boxes." How you choose to stay in touch will depend on your personal preferences and the culture of your organisation. And, as we saw in Class 7 (when we discovered that you have to be interest*ed* to be interest*ing*), you also need to be tuned into what's happening in the wider world. In fact, a CEO's antennae must have a range that stretches far beyond the company—starting with the board.

"I think it's extremely important that the CEO is continuously communicating with the board," says Abdel F. Badwi (Canada, Bankers Petroleum). "Not just at the board meeting but in between. The issues are more extensive than you can cover in a three or four hour meeting. If your board members are fully appraised of your business, ideas and plans, it's a lot easier to have them on side when it comes to decision making and healthy debate in the boardroom."

Perhaps this is all the more difficult, as it's something you rarely have to do before becoming CEO, when you probably reported to a single boss. Managing upwards and managing outwards are two very difficult activities, even though they draw on the same skills. Having a mentor who has experience of the reality of the CEO's position can be a great help. It can also help to deal with the challenge that all CEOs face at some point during their tenure: feeling alone.

8.2   Challenge 2: Coping with Loneliness

Richard Rushton explains: "It is quite a lonely job and does require introspection, but I believe in mentoring as a way of growing successful CEOs. I think that mentors who previously acted as CEOs in corporations can play an incredibly valuable role in helping with varied challenges and pressures.

A mentor from another industry can provide the seasoned CEO with new experiences and perspectives."

Jean Sentenac (France, Axens) is in full agreement. "Beyond your close colleagues, I think it's important in that position to have someone you can trust and you can talk to freely, without being afraid to do so—so as not to be alone," he says.

You can even kill two birds with one stone, by choosing your ex-CEO mentor from your own board. In fact, this is what Sentenac suggests: "It can be your Chairman, a board member, just as well as another adviser or coach." However, if there's no independent director with whom you can be completely honest and open, it may be better to look beyond the company board for your sounding board. "Sometimes you have to confront yourself from outside your organisation to check that what you're thinking is right—with someone who is not judging you but helping you," explains Sentenac.

Above all, your mentor, whether official or unofficial, board member or not, is your reality check. And the longer you stay in post, the more important that becomes. "The very big danger with long-serving CEOs is that they start to believe their own stories," concludes Rushton.

8.3   CHALLENGE 3: CONTINUING TO LEARN AND DEVELOP

For several of our interviewees, there is only one way to achieve longevity—and that's (you may have guessed it) to carry on learning. Whether it's the natural curiosity we saw in Class 2, the training to harness that curiosity through education we encountered in Class 3, the learning from experience of Class 4, the systematic self-directed learning of Class 5 or the "taking an interest" of Class 7, the ability to learn has been like a golden thread that runs through CEO School from enrolment to graduation.

"The most important thing the CEO must do is to educate himself or herself," says Temel Kotil (Turkey, Turkish Airlines). "Day to day, on a yearly basis, he or she needs to learn and challenge old thinking. I believe there is no CEO that is fully developed. This is my tenth year here. In the beginning I was more upset if things didn't work well. I got angry immediately. But later I said: OK, so let's improve it." And Kotil insists that he is still learning new ways of behaving, as well as new ideas.

Peter Coleman (Australia, Woodside) was only three years into the job when we met him. "Every year I write down a list of things I wish to improve on," he told us. "Learning is a lifetime journey. We learn something every day, whether about ourselves or about others or about the business. Leadership and consistently strong, relevant leadership is, in my view, characterised by lifetime learning." This is why curiosity is so important as a character trait. "An inquisitive mind is willing to accept and explore different ways of doing things," explains Coleman. Three years later, as we write this book, he is still in the post.

Learning is hardly, as they say, rocket science. Yang Wansheng (China, China Machinery Engineering Corporation) told us simply: "I have a personal development plan for the year ahead." And, although not everyone we spoke to had a formal learning schedule, there's no reason why the kind of professional and development plan you may have had as a more junior executive (see Classes 4 and 5) shouldn't continue. It can still include short programmes at business schools—but at a higher level than before. There are now many such courses specifically designed to help CEOs step back from the daily grind and consider their work from afar. Indeed, this is how we first met Mazen Khayyat (Saudi Arabia, El-Khayyat Group), who attended classes at INSEAD some years back.

Similarly, industry forums may have an increasingly important role to play as your tenure progresses. "I would say being really involved in your industry is important, through things like conferences and professional organisations," says Jean Sentenac. It's just that they may be different forums from those you attended before. And, as your free time dwindles, you may find your involvement more sporadic.

As Richard Rushton confirms, the time pressures of life as a CEO can change the way you learn. "I found my reading habits have changed, from reading books to articles," he says. "I read quickly on a number of topics, typically in the evenings."

Now that you're the boss, you also have access to new ways of honing your leadership capacities. "We've founded a group of CEOs in Korea and in it we share our working experiences," says Chul-Kyoon Lee of Daelim Industrial Co.

"This can be done by being involved in other boards, so that the successful CEO can see how other leaders and other board members are behaving," says Abdel F. Badwi, suggesting an alternative for those who don't have the option of joining a club of the kind described by Chul-Kyoon Lee. Once you have the title "CEO" on your business card, you'll be surprised how many invitations you receive to become a non-executive director of other organisations. And, depending on your schedule and interests, we'd advise you to accept one or maximum two of them. "Exposure to situations other than your own is the best schooling," continues Badwi. "I strongly encourage CEOs to be involved on other boards if they can, even if they are boards of non-profits. All will bring different interactions and enhance your communication skills."

As some of our co-authors suggested, one of the best ways for a CEO to learn is, strangely enough, to teach others. As Vladimir Rashevsky (Russia, SUEK) so neatly puts it: "By educating others, you educate yourself—expanding your knowledge and deepening your expertise."

Becoming a CEO gives you a learning and development "makeover." *Before*, you simply learned from others. *After*, the boundaries between teaching and learning are blurred. You can learn from teaching your direct reports, other employees in your company, students at business schools or even pupils at your kids' high school. The wider your "student circle," the more you will discover. And, by the way, you don't need to become a CEO to start doing this!

8.4   CHALLENGE 4: KNOWING WHEN TO GO

Assuming you actually do become a CEO, the day will inevitably arrive when you start to feel you have learned all there is to learn. This is a sure sign that you have reached the final stage in the CEO lifecycle: decline.

The Three Ages of the CEO
Some people say that a CEO's tenure has three phases. But the trick is to avoid phase three altogether… just like the third envelope in our opening joke.

Phase One: Entry
The lifecycle starts with a "honeymoon" period, when the new leader defines her project (or "plot" as John Browne, ex-CEO of BP, liked to call it), puts together a team, deepens her knowledge of the industry and the organisation, and generally learns the ropes. This is an exciting—and precarious—time filled with new ideas, experiments, mistakes, insights and discoveries. The company's performance is still largely defined by the previous CEO's decisions, and the incomer's self-confidence fluctuates from high to low on an hourly basis.

(continued)

(continued)

Phase Two: Maturity

When the main choices have been made and self-confidence has sta-
bilised, the real change begins. The new CEO is firmly in control
and enters the second stage of the lifecycle: maturity. Maturity does
not mean boredom, though. If anything, the work is even more
exciting. The CEO feels she has mastered her job, and the company
performance proves it. At the same time, the leader continues to
learn, the competitive environment evolves—and so the organisational vision evolves too—but the main elements of the CEO's original project remain.

Phase Three: Decline

Some exceptional people—like Jack Welch of GE, Steve Jobs of
Apple or Herman Gref of Sberbank—have managed to live through
more than one "CEO project" in the same company, radically changing its focus, strategy, product portfolio, values and senior managers.
But most CEOs enter the decline stage, once their main goals have
been achieved or become irrelevant, core ideas have been imple-
mented or rejected, and major investment projects have been realised
or discontinued. During the decline, CEOs may become complacent
or lose focus. Typically, their passion for business disappears, and
thirst for new knowledge diminishes. If they go deep into this stage,
other people begin to notice, morale drops and eventually the company performance suffers.

There is no consensus on the "right" term of office for a CEO. Some
of our co-authors have been in their seats for more than a decade. Jeffrey
Immelt has been leading General Electric for 17 years, and Vladimir
Rashevsky, though still only 43, has been in charge of SUEK for 14 years.
Temel Kotil has resigned after 11 years as a boss of Turkish Airlines, and
Diego Bolzonello stepped down as CEO of Geox after 17 years. However,
as we saw at the very beginning of this book, the "100 best performing
CEOs in the world" (according to *Harvard Business Review*) have an
average tenure of twelve years and keep going, while the average CEO of
a large public company spends less than four years in post.

Good CEOs shorten the entry stage of the lifecyle by doing a lot of prep-
work beforehand, but this is only possible if their succession has been

planned long in advance. And even in the best-planned cases, it takes time for a newcomer to become fully operational. Boards and investors are well aware of this fact and allow new CEOs some period of grace. Their real challenge is to help CEOs to leave on time. However, the decline stage usually kicks in before its outward signs become visible. So to it falls on the CEO's shoulders to leave the stage while still operating at peak performance.

So how do you know when to go? We believe the healthy length of a CEO's term is a function of many variables: the company's size and complexity; the industry's investment cycles (sectors like mining or energy tend to require longer tenures); the shareholders' investment horizon and appetite for risk; the CEO's scale of ambition, level of energy and capacity to learn (and unlearn); and, of course, market conjecture. In today's complex yet fast-changing world, anything less than three years seems too short for a CEO of any sizeable company while anything over a decade begins to look risky.

There are two strategies to choose for deciding when to step down. The majority of the CEOs we know select the first: when you feel like it. The minority opt for the second: the moment when your successor is ready. Needless to say, a significant number do not think about this question at all. One survey showed that almost 30% of the CEOs of American companies would like to die in office. And no, this is not another joke! We believe that the most productive approach is to depart when your successor is ready. However, it's equally important not to stay beyond a certain date that has been defined well in advance and shared with important stakeholders. This strategy puts the onus on the incumbent CEO to prepare a successor yet, at the same time, mitigates the risk of using "she is not ready yet" as an excuse for staying for ever.

8.5   CHALLENGE 5: PLANNING YOUR FUTURE, AS WELL AS YOUR SUCCESSION

Choosing and preparing a successor is a daunting task, so it can be tempting to forget an equally important mission: planning your own future. By virtue of the kind of people they are, however (see Class 7), ex-CEOs rarely stop working completely. Not only for you own benefit but for the benefit of your successor, you need to define your post-CEO life and start to prepare for it while you are grooming the next boss to take over. The opportunities are plentiful: entrepreneurship, investments, non-executive directorships, advisory roles, public jobs and even academic posts. You may not like what you have chosen when you try it, but you need to have a concrete strategy for your future. Our own consulting work and research show that CEOs without specific "retirement" plans are likely to prolong their tenure beyond its sell-by date by using a range of different excuses.

One final word of wisdom: do not hang around the company after leaving the CEO job. Many outgoing leaders try to stay on as advisors, board members or even chairs of the board, citing the need to ensure a smooth transition to the new leader. This is an admirable sentiment, but we say: ensure that smooth transition while you are still in post. The day your successor moves into the corner office, stop looking over her shoulder and casting your shadow over the company. And if you're reluctant to take our advice, consider the research. Studies clearly demonstrate that, when the outgoing CEO becomes the chair at the same company, on average its performance deteriorates and the new CEO does not stay long. If the new leader needs you, she will let you know. Otherwise, don't interfere!

By the way, everything said above applies to other senior executive successions not only the CEO's. So sit up and take notice! Even if you are not in the top job yet, our advice may help you to get there.

But if you are among the lucky few who have already made it to CEO and you're determined to make a successful exit, start looking for a worthy replacement right now (if you haven't already done so). To borrow from the great Jack Welch, this is "the most important decision in your life." Before sailing off into the sunset on your ex-CEO yacht, take a moment to go back to the beginning of this book and define the profile of your successor.

Here's a quick checklist summarising all our classes so far to help you.

Checklist for Choosing a CEO

Personality traits
Must have:
[] Curiosity
[] Ambition
[] Passion

Education
Nice to have but not essential:
[] A good degree from a well-respected institution
[] An MBA

(*continued*)

(continued)

Experience
As many of the following as possible:
[] Work across several functions
[] In-depth expertise in a single function
[] International CV
[] Managing adversity early

Must have:
[] P&L responsibility
[] Long and diverse experience of managing people
[] Industry knowledge—and preferably company-specific knowledge

Skills
Must be capable of:
[] C-thinking (complex, critical, creative and constructive)
[] E-acumen (emotional—especially empathetic—acumen)
[] O-learning (ongoing openness to operationalisation of learning of
all kinds, including self-knowledge)

Suitability for the following roles
*Must demonstrate ability to do **all** of the following:*
[] Envisioning a future that will inspire others
[] Nominating the right people to implement the vision
[] Enabling those people to do their job
[] Crisis management

Style
Must exude the following:
[] Company champion
[] Global mindset
[] Interesting and interested person
[] Healthy lifestyle
[] Disciplined and organised approach

CHAPTER 9

Conclusion: Lessons for Future Ceos, Their Parents and Educators

Abstract We conclude by reviewing the implications of CEO School for our various audiences. We remind aspiring Ceos of the need to take their physical condition very seriously; to make sure their levels of ambition, passion and curiosity are high; to settle on the industry of their choice; and to keep on developing CEO skills. Their parents can help by giving them every possible chance to develop CAP, systemic thinking, emotional acumen and desire to learn from an early age. There are similar lessons for teachers—from kindergarten to high school. Foster curiosity, enthusiasm and collaboration, whatever age group or subject you teach. Meanwhile, business school professors (ourselves included) should examine their own curricula and lesson plans. Are we really teaching the subjects relevant to future business leaders?

People who are empowered to select future Ceos—board members and business owners—should define precisely what they are looking for, rely on collective wisdom rather than one person's judgement and apply a variety of techniques to assess future business leaders.

Keywords Board of directors • Business schools • Educators • MBA curriculum • Parents

Jadilah kumbang, hidup sekali di taman bunga, jangan jadi lalat, hidup sekali di bukit sampah. (Indonesia)
    Meaning: Life is what you make of it.

© The Author(s) 2018
S. Shekshnia et al., *CEO School*,
https://doi.org/10.1007/978-981-10-7865-1_9

To some extent our survey of 20 global CEOs confirmed what we already knew about effective business leadership. Our interviewees echoed the conclusions of many academic researchers. That is, it's preferable to recruit the next leader from within the company and certainly the same industry; cognitive and social skills are critical for effective performance; and CEOs should be able to formulate a vision, appoint talented people and help them to succeed. They also confirmed that formal education per se is not a prerequisite for success.

However, we also encountered several unorthodox findings along the way. Our CEOs' overwhelming emphasis on curiosity and learning in all its forms was unexpected. And we didn't suppose we'd find such similarities between the attitudes of CEOs from different cultures—or that they'd play down the importance of international exposure for future business leaders (although their insistence on a global *outlook* and *openness* to diverse ways of seeing the world came as no surprise).

Perhaps, the most important insight for us was that successful CEOs do not consider their job enormously complex. They speak about it in understandable terms and suggest comprehensive but simple ways of getting it done.

We believe the checklist on the previous page, and the insights that it summarises are worth sitting up and taking notice of. After all, the CEOs who supplied them will be looking for precisely these attributes in their successors. So what are the implications for you? Well, that depends on your personal motivation for reading this book in the first place.

9.1   FOR ASPIRING CEOS

Take a good long look at yourself. If our CEOs are to be believed, anyone who has passed the age of 20 and is not curious, ambitious *and* passionate should consider an alternative career plan. If just one of these is missing from your make-up, it may already be too late. Of course, you can work on growing your CAP capital, as we described in Class 2, but these three personality traits are best developed in childhood and may even—to some extent—be inborn. That's the bad news. The good news, on the other hand (from Class 3), is that a top degree from an elite institution is not essential (though it may give you a head start).

Assuming you have curiosity, ambition and passion in abundance, you should settle on an industry of your choice as soon as possible and immerse yourself in its methods and its culture. Specialise in one discipline, but also seek out as much breadth as possible for your CV. Seize early opportunities for managing both people and P&L, and work on the three key CEO skills (C-thinking, E-acumen and O-learning) while gaining as much practice in CEO-like roles as possible (remember particularly what we learned in Classes 4–6).

Perhaps most important of all, take your physical condition very seriously. Systematically look after your health and try to balance the professional elements of your life with hobbies, family, friends or all three (Class 7). When you're a CEO, realistically, you won't have much time for them, so it's essential that you figure out what (outside of work) counts most in your world.

9.2 For Educators of Future CEOs

As we said at the outset, education begins at home. Parents who want to provide their children with the widest range of opportunities in life should give them every possible chance to develop CAP, systemic thinking, emotional acumen and desire to learn. By making time to talk with your children from an early age, providing them with household responsibilities, giving them chances to participate in decision-making, introducing them to competitive sports, ensuring they make the best educational choices, encouraging experimentation and facilitating collaboration with other people, you will make a positive impact on your children's preparedness for a leadership role.

Whoever heard of a kid that wanted to grow up to be a CEO, anyway? Train driver, rock star, ballet dancer, astronaut, footballer, inventor... these are dreams of childhood. Yet the qualities and skills required to play the roles we have described in this book will come in handy for most fields of human endeavour. So, whatever your own ambitions for your children, encourage them to have a dream, to explore the world, to develop passions, to learn from people and experiences, to interact with other kids and adults and—above all—to understand themselves. Understanding what makes human beings tick will stand them in good stead, whatever they decide they want to do in life.

There are similar lessons for teachers—from kindergarten to high school. Foster curiosity, enthusiasm and collaboration, whatever age group or subject you teach. Encourage your pupils to have grand ambitions for themselves, as well as to formulate big ideas that will inspire others to follow. Give them opportunities to decide, to experiment and to make mistakes. Then help them to learn from those mistakes.

Meanwhile, business school professors (ourselves included) should examine their own curricula and lesson plans. Are we really teaching the subjects relevant to future business leaders? Developing vision, selecting talent, enabling performance, managing in a crisis, personal discipline, balanced techniques... are these on the syllabus? Or are we burying them so deep in traditional disciplines, such as strategy, operations, marketing and organisational behaviour that students don't realise they're there? Worse still, are we teaching pointlessly complex frameworks of leadership, such as "cognitive maps," "unambiguous signalling of intentions" or "unconscious intrapsychic dynamics?"

Clearly, not everyone who enrols at business school is destined to become a CEO. But all students would benefit from some "CEO training" in subjects that haven't traditionally been taught. How to learn and unlearn at all stages of your career, how to be healthy and how to find and maintain your personal style... some business schools are already experimenting with these as learning objectives. Unfortunately, they're not best achieved through the traditional lectures and case studies, which means many business schools back away from innovating in leadership development.

Even if leadership development falls outside of the professorial comfort zone, MBA teachers shouldn't leave it to chance or dismiss it as too expensive to do properly. Such methods as individual and group coaching, role-playing simulations or online games—followed by reflection sessions—are proven to make a strong impact on the development of leadership skills. With the new fashion for "flipping the classroom" (delivering content before the session, then using the learning to complete practical exercises during the session), leadership development could even be integrated across the entire curriculum.

Given our CEOs' insistence on the desirability of industry knowledge, we would also like to suggest that business schools start teaching hard skills, perhaps in partnership with technical universities or maybe creative colleges. These institutions can provide training in state-of-the-art technology and services to supplement the training in *managing* technology and services traditionally provided as part of MBA programmes. Such partnerships would make business schools much more attractive to aspiring and practising CEOs.

Last but not least, business schools should help people think about the CEO's job so that students can assess their potential, make an evidence-based decision for targeting it and develop a specific plan to achieve their ambition. INSEAD and its Global Leadership Center have started on this road by developing assessment instruments, collecting and analysing data on thousands of high-potential and high-achieving executives, conducting group and individual coaching sessions and helping participants to prepare and implement personal development plans. To become even more relevant for future CEOs, this work should focus increasingly on the attributes that current CEOs themselves consider critical for their success.

9.3   FOR SELECTORS OF CEOS

We hope that this book will help people involved in selecting CEOs, whether board members, business owners, headhunters, HR professionals, consultants or incumbent CEOs. The first insight for them comes from Diego Bolzonello of Geox (Italy) who insists that good selection decisions cannot be made single-handed: "Without a team you couldn't say if this could be a good CEO. There are so many skills that you have to understand that one person cannot understand them all. It would be very risky from my point of view. Can he understand a balance sheet? Is she an expert in the product and organisation? Is he a leader? You need a group of people that are used to making this kind of decision."

However, the fact remains that the "human" skills we've seen throughout this book are very difficult to assess, unless you've worked alongside the candidate concerned. First impressions are notoriously misleading, and interviews are a famously blunt-edged tool for assessing leadership ability.

"How to treat people? How to treat customers? How to make them comfortable?" asks Stefan Messer (Germany, Messer Group) "This can be so different depending on the people you're working with. You may have very good people with a very good education, but they fall down because they don't know how to treat their secretary or the other employees. We have interviews for that, of course, and we observe them, how they behave, how they tell their story." He laughs wryly, before concluding, "We still make a lot of mistakes!"

Our second recommendation is therefore that CEO selectors use a variety of techniques for reaching a final decision, perhaps even observing how candidates behave during tours of the shop floor. Formal interactive assessment methods can also be very helpful. "What we've used in the past is a kind of business game," says Jean Sentenac (France, Axens). "We've simulated a situation and the person had to make decisions. It was a way to check reactions and to start a discussion."

Mazen Khayyat (Saudi Arabia, El-Khayyat Group) also recommends the use of case studies in assessing the harder skills of future CEOs—not just "to see the way they analyse information and make decisions based on it" but to give a better insight into financial background. In short, no one is too senior to be tested in this way. And how better to test the CEO roles of Class 6 than through a spot of role-playing?

Our third insight is that you need to know what you are looking for. Since your chances of finding an all-round perfect candidate—a "Renaissance man" in the words of Vladimir Rashevsky of SUEK (Russia)—are slim, you have to decide on what is a must and where you can compromise. This book provides a profile of an ideal candidate: a person with high CAP, consummate social skills, an eye for the whole as well as the parts, the ability to learn from any situation, boundless enthusiasm for the company, compassion, empathy, physical fitness and self-discipline. And the checklist at the beginning of this chapter offers a solid foundation for each CEO-selecting team (we hope you are convinced that it has to be a team) to add a couple of characteristics specific to your company at this point in its development.

CEO adviser and best-selling author Ram Charan calls these extras the "pivot" that will make all the difference to your organisation. It could consist of "passion for digital technology and global experience" for a bank with ambitions for international expansion from an emerging country. Or it might be "customer-orientation, lateral thinking and a knack for collaboration" for an 80-year-old steel giant from a traditional industrial region. What we have described in this book is necessary but not sufficient. The pivot is critical but will not work without a solid foundation. We hope that this advice will help CEO recruiters identify candidates who have both—or at least a strong chance of developing what's missing.

Our fourth and final piece of advice is well known, but all too many companies ignore it and fall into the classic trap of selecting an improved version of the outgoing CEO. Admittedly, this approach has worked extremely well for one of the oldest companies in the world, Japanese hotel and spa, Hōshi Royakan. For the last 13 centuries, they have done exactly that—train the son of the owner-operator to be a better copy of his father. But your business is almost certainly nothing like Hōshi Royakan, which still provides pretty much the same hot spring spa services in the same location as it did in the year 718. The main reason companies change the CEO is… change. So forget about who is running your business today and think about who you need to run your business tomorrow. Define your strategic intent, formulate a pivot to ensure its success and look for a person who is the closest match.

9.4 Why Not a CEO School?

"Of course, it is not like a CEO needs to pass an admissions test," says Vladimir Rashevsky. So we don't propose to set up a CEO School or set a competitive entrance exam any time soon. What's more, some 90% of our 20 "co-authors" agreed that CEO is not a profession like any other. The kind of training that produces engineers, lawyers and doctors is simply not an option. But if there's one thing we've learned in the course of this book, it's that effective CEOs never stop learning.

Business schools, universities, consultants, publishers, companies and HR professionals must provide a wide selection of activities, information and experience designed to help develop the careers of business leaders. Aspiring and acting CEOs must choose wisely from among them. We hope that his book has been a helpful contribution. In the end, though, you will have to make your own CEO School.

CEO Bios

Abdel F. Badwi
Position: President and CEO of Bankers Petroleum Ltd. (2008–2013)
Location: Canada
Abdel F. Badwi is an international energy executive and professional geologist with more than 40 years' experience in the exploration, development and production of oil and gas fields in Europe, the Americas, Asia and the Middle East. Before joining Bankers Petroleum he was President and CEO of Rally Energy Corp., an oil and gas company with operations in Egypt and Pakistan, as well as Canada. He has also been a board member of several Canadian public and private companies. He holds a degree in geology from Alexandria University, Egypt.

Renato Bertani
Position: CEO, Barra Energia (2010–)
Location: Brazil
Renato Bertani has led Barra Energia since its foundation as an independent oil and gas exploration, development and production company based in Rio de Janeiro. He has nearly 40 years of international experience in oil exploration and production, and acquisitions and divestitures throughout the world. Bertani worked for 31 years at Petrobras, the Brazilian state oil company, and was subsequently CEO of Thompson & Knight Global Energy Services. He has also served as President of the World Petroleum Council. A graduate in geology from the University of Rio Grande do Sul,

© The Author(s) 2018
S. Shekshnia et al., *CEO School*,
https://doi.org/10.1007/978-981-10-7865-1

141

Brazil, with a PhD from the University of Illinois, USA, he is now a highly successful teacher of management, dedicated to passing on his experience to executives in the energy business.

Diego Bolzonello
Position: CEO, Geox (2002–2012)
Location: Italy
Working closely with the company's founder, Mario Moretti Polegato, Diego Bolzonello helped take Geox from a start-up with a good idea to one of the world's biggest shoe companies. The company's innovative "breathable shoe" technology, Polegato's passion for the business and Bolzonello's own expertise in managing growth through innovation proved to be an unbeatable combination. An economics graduate of the University of Venice, Bolzonello stepped down (shortly after being interviewed for this book) in 2012 and set up his own management consulting business.

Peter Coleman
Position: CEO and Managing Director, Woodside (2011–)
Location: Australia
Peter Coleman joined Woodside, Australia's largest independent oil and gas company, after 27 years of global experience with the ExxonMobil group. He began his career as a drilling engineer in his native Australia and rose steadily through the management ranks as he rotated around posts in the USA, Nigeria and Indonesia. He is a graduate in engineering and computing of Monash University with an MBA from Deakin University (both Melbourne) and remains actively involved in business education, particularly with the University of Western Australia (Perth).

Bob Dudley
Position: Group Chief Executive, BP (2010–)
Location: UK
Bob Dudley has spent his entire career in the oil and gas industry. He first entered the public consciousness during the Deepwater Horizon oil spill, when he deftly steered BP through the crisis—and was subsequently appointed as CEO. Under his leadership, BP has been transformed into a safer, stronger and simpler business. Dudley has worked in a variety of technical and management positions worldwide: first for Amoco, the company he originally joined as an MBA graduate, and—following the merger

of the two organisations in 1998—for BP. He holds a degree in chemical engineering from the University of Illinois and an MBA from Southern Methodist University (both in the USA).

Constantino Galanis
Position: General Director, Química Apollo (1987–)
Location: Mexico
Constantino Galanis has made two major moves in this life. First, he emigrated from Greece to the USA with his family at the age of 14. Second, he moved from the USA to Mexico with the company he had joined straight out of Rutgers University, where he studied environmental engineering and business administration. Today, Química Apollo is an industrial organic chemicals manufacturer, headquartered in Mexico and supplying the energy sector. Galanis worked his way up through a range of technical and commercial roles to CEO, and the company has thrived under his long leadership. Although he has had many job offers from elsewhere, he feels an immense sense of solidarity with his adopted country and the organisation to which he has dedicated his entire career.

Miguel Galuccio
Position: CEO, YPF (2012–2016)
Location: Argentina
Miguel Galuccio was appointed CEO of Argentina's national oil company, when it was taken back into partial state ownership in 2012. During his tenure, YPF grew significantly in terms of investments, profitability and reserves, helping to make Argentina the world's second biggest producer of shale gas. Galuccio had in fact begun his career in the organisation, following his studies in petroleum engineering at the Institute of Technology of Buenos Aires, but had left in 1999 following its privatisation and acquisition by a Spanish company. He subsequently made his name at Schlumberger, where he is now a board member. He resigned from his post as CEO of YPF after a change of government.

Jeffrey Immelt
Position: CEO, General Electric Company (2001–), and Chairman until 2017
Location: USA
One of the world's most well-known business leaders, Jeffrey Immelt makes frequent appearances in rankings of the best, most admired and most influential CEOs. He acted as an economic and business adviser to

the Obama administration and is today perhaps even more famous than his predecessor at GE, Jack Welch. Immelt obtained a BA in applied mathematics from Dartmouth College and an MBA from Harvard Business School, before joining GE, where his father had managed one of the divisions. He worked in various parts of the group in increasingly senior roles, until he was finally appointed to replace Welch in September 2001, just four days before the 9/11 terrorist attacks.

Shuzo Kaihori
Position: CEO, Yokogawa Electric Corporation (2008–2015), now Chairman of the Board
Location: Japan
Shuzo Kaihori began his career at Yokogawa in 1973, following a masters in engineering at Keio University. He has been with the company ever since. During the early part of his long career, he chiefly worked on the industrial automation and control side of the business, focusing on technology, engineering and services. Later he served as President of the company's US operations and was appointed COO of the entire group before moving on to become CEO and eventually Chairman of the Board, as part of a carefully managed succession process.

Mazen Khayyat
Position: General Manager, El-Khayyat Group (2004–)
Location: Saudi Arabia
El-Khayyat Group is a holding company operating across a range of sectors in Saudi Arabia and beyond. It employs more than 2,800 people across 24 countries and 4 continents and has embarked on multiple international joint ventures. Mazen Khayyat, the son of the founder, is following—and expanding on—his father's vision. With degrees in engineering and engineering management from George Washington University, USA, Khayyat returned home to Saudi Arabia and worked in the group's construction companies, before taking overall responsibility for the company and its future.

Temel Kotil
Position: President and CEO, Turkish Airlines (2005–2016)
Location: Turkey
Temel Kotil's trajectory to the top of one of the world's great flag carriers was unconventional. After a degree in aeronautical engineering at Istanbul Technical University, he completed a PhD at the University of Michigan,

Ann Arbor. An academic career followed, but eventually Kotil decided to deploy his research and engineering skills in business, as head of research, planning and coordination at Advanced Innovative Technologies Inc., New York. On returning to Turkey, he joined Turkish Airlines as the leader of technical affairs, before being appointed as CEO in 2005. During his tenure the company experienced extraordinary growth and was ranked the best airline in Europe for four years in row.

Chul-Kyoon Lee
Position: President and CEO, Daelim Industrial Co. (2014–2016)
Location: South Korea
The history of Daelim Industrial Co. is closely entwined with that of the nation's construction industry—and the construction of a great industrial nation. With a focus on cutting-edge technology and innovation, as well as social responsibility, the company was one of South Korea's pioneers in serving overseas markets. Chul-Kyoon Lee joined the organisation after studying mechanical engineering at Yongsan Technical High School, and his career grew with the company, which is now a global leader in engineering construction with an annual operating income of more than US$250 million.

Stefan Messer
Position: CEO, Messer Group (2004–)
Location: Germany
Messer Group was founded by Stefan Messer's grandfather in 1898 and—though he joined the company soon after graduating in economics from the University of Mannheim in 1976—he had to lead a buyout to take back control of the company in 2004. Having worked in Messer subsidiaries in Austria, France and the Netherlands, he knew the organisation inside out and was the obvious choice to steer it out of a financially perilous situation. Messer Group is now wholly family owned once again with approximately 5,500 employees and total sales of over €1 billion annually.

Vladimir Rashevsky
Position: CEO, SUEK (2004–)
Location: Russia
Vladimir Rashevsky began his career in banking, after graduating from the Moscow's Financial University with a degree in economics. In 2004 he made the switch from finance to coal, joining SUEK, first as President and then as CEO. Today, the company is one of the world's top ten coal

producers by output, national sales and reserves—and the largest in Russia. During Rashevsky's tenure, it has also diversified into logistics, investing in three major ports. In addition, under his leadership, the organisation is also actively involved in social and charitable projects for the regions in which it operates.

Richard Rushton
Position: Managing Director, Distell Group Limited (2013–)
Location: South Africa
Richard Rushton has had an illustrious global career in the beverage industry. With SABMiller, he worked in general management positions in Botswana, India, Ecuador and Colombia, before returning to his native South Africa to take the top job at Distell. The company is now Africa's largest producer of alcoholic beverages with a portfolio of brands in cider, wine and spirits—and some 5,500 employees. Under Rushton's leadership, the company has expanded into new markets and continued to post strong results, despite tough economic conditions. He holds a degree in business and economic management from the University of the Witwatersrand, Johannesburg.

José Ángel Sánchez
Position: Director General of Real Madrid (2011–)
Location: Spain
Before becoming the "CEO" of Real Madrid, José Ángel Sánchez was a senior marketing executive at the club for 11 years. He is known as one of the top business managers in the footballing world—largely responsible for turning Real Madrid into the highly profitable machine it is today through his expertise in marketing and economics. He has also played a key role in high-profile signings, including David Beckham, Cristiano Ronaldo and Ricardo Kaká. A graduate in philosophy from the Complutense University of Madrid, Sánchez began his career in retail, before moving on to the computer games industry and rising to become Director General and CEO of Sega for Southern Europe.

Jean Sentenac
Position: President and CEO, Axens (2002–)
Location: France
Jean Sentenac graduated from France's elite École Polytechnique and also holds a postgraduate engineering degree from IFP School, part of the French Institute of Petroleum. He began his career in engineering and

construction with Air Liquide in Spain and Italy, followed by ten years of experience in the chemical industry with Rhône-Poulenc and Rhodia. He joined Axens as Deputy CEO and was promoted to the top job in 2002. Since then, Sentenac has guided the development and growth of Axens as a leading supplier to clients in the hydrocarbon process industries.

Didie Soewondho
Position: Chairman and CEO, PT Wijaya Infrastruktur Indonesia
Location: Indonesia
Didie Soewondho is one of Indonesia's leading entrepreneurs and an expert on domestic and international geopolitics, trade, investment and finance. He also plays a major role in the Indonesian Chamber of Commerce and Industry and the Indonesia-Russia Business Council. As well as leading a major infrastructure company, he has other business interests, including founding an IT company that makes mobile apps for the Indonesian police force.

Nishi Vasudeva
Position: Chairman and Managing Director, Hindustan Petroleum Corporation (2014–2016)
Location: India
The first woman to lead an Indian petroleum company, Nishi Vasudeva has long experience in the industry—covering marketing, planning, strategy and information systems. In 2015, she was honoured as both global CEO of the Year and Asia CEO of the Year by Platts Global Energy Awards, the "Oscars" of the industry. She effectively turned around the part state-owned, part publicly listed company, delivering an increase in over 200% in stock market value during her first year on the job. During her tenure, the company also reported record profits, despite challenging market conditions. Vasudeva obtained an MBA and postgraduate diploma from the Indian Institute of Management, Kolkata. Since retiring, she has remained active in business through directorships of several companies.

Yang Wansheng
Position: Chairman and Executive Director, China Machinery Engineering Corporation (2010–2013)
Location: China
Yang Wansheng dedicated much career to the state-owned China Machinery Engineering Corporation. An active Communist Party of China member, he originally joined the organisation in 1982, leaving only

to study in the USA in 1990. On his return to China, he took a government post relating to the machinery industry, before rejoining the company in 1999. He was finally appointed to the top job in 2010. Yang graduated from the Beijing Second Foreign Language College in 1979 and holds a masters in management science from MIT.

INDEX

© The Author(s) 2018   149
S. Shekshnia et al., *CEO School*,
https://doi.org/10.1007/978-981-10-7865-1

Lightning Source UK Ltd.
Milton Keynes UK
UKHW02f1324050418

320562UK00005B/643/P

9 789811 078644